Poetic Tales from St. Kilda

by

Colin Demét

© Copyright 2006 Colin Demét.

All rights reserved. No part of this publication may be reproduced, stored in a retrieval system, or transmitted, in any form or by any means, electronic, mechanical, photocopying, recording, or otherwise, without the written prior permission of the author.

Published by Wordcatcher Publications in 2006

Printed in the Isle of Lewis.

A catalogue record for this book
is available from the British Library

ISBN -10
0-9551318-1-2

ISBN -13
978-0-9551318-1-3

Cover: Photograph by Captain F.W.L. Thomas. R.N.
Taken from the book
St. Kilda Past and Present by George Seaton (1878)

Printed and bound on the Isle of Lewis by
Wordcatcher Publications
Loch á Tuath Cottage
Flesherin, Point,
Isle of Lewis, HS2 0HE

www.wordcatcherpublications.com

CONTENTS

Acknowledgements

	Page
SKILDIR	9
The Lonely Lady	10
55 Million Years B.C.	12
Amuinn a Ghlinne Mhoir	14
Ruaival to Oiseval	15
Coachair	15
Sea-girt Isle	16
The Summit Ridge	16
Stacked Stacs Crowned Pinnacles	17
Stac Soay	17
Stac Biorach	17
Stac Dona	17
Stac Am Plastair	18
Stac an Armin	18
Stac Lee	19
Boreray	19
Soay	21
The Tunnel	21
The Dùn Passage	22
3000 Years BC	23
Beauty and the Beast	29
The Galley	31
The Amazon House and the Amazon Queen	33
Sgàthach and Aoife	36
The Sinking of the Crown	38
From Gleann Mór to Village Bay	39
HIORT	
The Earth-House 'House of Fairies' Tigh an t'sithiche.	
500 B.C. – 300A.D.	40
Calum Mor's House. 600 A.D.	42
The Bee-hive Annexe	44
All Remains the Same	45
The Vikings Funeral	47
The Ghost of Lady Grange	50
Dun-Fir-Bholg	51
Hökunótt	53

HIRTA

The Old Village 1615 *(March 7ᵗʰ)*	55
The Mistress Stone	57
The Well of Youth	57
The Wedding	60
The Wedding Dance	62
The Coll MacDonald Raid 1615 *(April 15ᵗʰ)*	
The outlaw Coll Ciotach (Ketoch alías Macgillespick)	64
Coll MacDonald and the Ancient Villager	67
Friends	68
Utopia	69

ST. KILDA

The Beginning of the End	
Regeneration —— Utopia	71
The Black Prince	72
Leprosy 1684	74
Roderick the Imposter 1697	75
Martin Martin's visit 1697 *(1ˢᵗ June)*	78
The Calends Yelling	81
The Bannock Cake Barley Wine Dance	83
The Cavalcade	84
The Cragsmen	85

TALES FROM THE CARDING PARTIES

	90
The Gift O' the Gab	91
The Changeling	94
The Water Bull	97
The Well of Youth	102
The Stone of Knowledge	104
The Milking Stone	105
On Sea and On Land	106
The Burning of the Church	107
The Cave of the Irishman	110
The Seal Woman	111
The Empty Carding Room	116
The Reverend Alexander Buchan 1705	118
Will-O'-The-Wisp	119
Smallpox 1727	121
Marooned on Stac an Armin 1728 *(May 13ᵗʰ)*	122
Bonnie Prince Charlie 1746 *(April)*	124

The Hunting of the Prince 1746 *(June 20ʰ)*	126
The Laird of Islay and Marion Gillies 1799	129
Marion's Lament	130
The Apostle of the North 1822 *(September 16ʰ)*	132
The Great Auk	134
Reverend Neil Mackenzie 1829	138
Reverend John Mackay 1865	139
The Queen of St. Kilda	140
Lockjaw. Tetanus Infantum. The Sickness of Eight Days	141
The Knee Woman	142
Dunara Castle. The Tourists 1877 *(July 2ⁿ)*	143
The Marriage of Annie Ferguson to Neil Gillies 1890	146
The New Queen of St. Kilda	146
The Mini Mail Boats	149
Hunger 1912	150
Influenza Epidemic 1913	151
War 1914	152
The Petition 1930 *(May 10ʰ)*	153
The Last People from the Edge of the World Village Bay 1930 *(June)*	
Visiting the Houses. Numbers 1 to 16	154
The Drowning of the Dogs	168
The Evacuation of St Kilda 1930 *(August, Wednesday 29ʰ)*	169

ILLUSTRATIONS

	Page
Map of St. Kilda *(From a survey by J. Norman Heathcote)*	13
The Black Prince *(Line engraving, published in "Harper's Weekly", 1866)*	73

The following plates are from the 1878 publication of St. Kilda Past and Present by George Seaton.

St. Kilda Cragsmen	86
St. Kilda Man	89
St. Kilda Women	117
East Bay with Conagher	127
The Great Auk	136

ACKNOWLEDGEMENTS

We would like to thank the people from the reference and historical department of the Stornoway Library for their kind and helpful assistance.

*I awoke to find I was sleeping.
It was dark yet the room was light.
I knew where I was, yet I was somewhere else.
The Wordcatcher sleeps tonight.*

SKILDIR

Floating high above the sea
Shield domes float far below
White-washed tears twinkle, winking eye
I hear a roar 'SKILDIR'
The mighty Viking cry.

Heersht......Heersht......Heersht
Waves gently caressing sands salt kiss
Waiting at the edge of time
Voices whispering sighs sublime
Return, Spirit fly free Great Auk
The beak scream shrill screech cry... Hiort

Through silent noise, peace rage? Birth, Death.
I shake my head to wake. No escape.
Voices! Secrets ride the whispering winds
I cry 'Please! Let me go?' 'NO'
The time has come for all to know.

Heersht......Heersht......Heersht
Whispering waves
From sands salt kiss

I awoke, into a foreboding silence. . . . . . I spoke aloud to myself, '**OH NO** not again, where am I now?' There was a faint, relaxing sound in the distance, like ... like ... *whispering* ... like hundreds of voices *whispering* ... like ... gentle waves stroking the sleeping sands of a beach. I suddenly jumped, startled by a woman's voice whispering into my ear. *"We have been waiting a long time for you, welcome to Hiort, the sighing of the sea, and the tales from the island of St Kilda".*

I turned my head toward the voice and facing me was the lonely lady's face; the face I had seen many times whilst travelling 'The Winged Isle'. She had never spoken to me in the past, and now I realized why. She had been waiting for my arrival on St. Kilda. I recalled part of the poem I had written about her from *'Poetic Tales from the Isle of Skye'* for this lady's sorrow was as I have never before seen nor known.

THE LONELY LADY

I never knew your name
For naught to me you tell
I saw your face in a deep dark night
'Twas shining back from hell.

Your hair was red like fire
Weaving flames to lick a hand close by
And all the time a constant hiss
Tears kiss the flames to cry.

Your eyes were sad and lost
Abandoned lonely
Void and blank
I tried to catch a fleeting glance
All hope be lost to chance.

Many times return Wordcatcher,
So sad, to help, to know,
Yet nothing in the eyes was seen
Where barren flowers grow.

Sometimes shadows passed by
Memories lost, floating, brief,
A wind to blow lost green dreams
The breeze blown crisp brown leaf.

Never a soul so lonely lost
As if some living dead
A lady's heart destroyed
Her spirit thread-bare bled.

The pieces of a jigsaw seen
Float one sometimes another
So hard to catch a long time past
Old ghosts forever hover.

[From Poetic Tales from the Isle of Skye]

Wordcatcher

Who are you?
Your face! The pain!
And yet, such strength
Why do you remain?
And suffer so
Your aching bones
A flickering light
Remaining for to fight, for?
Some battle, restless spirit?
A woman scorned revenge?
Compensation?
Requital?
Retaliation?
HA! Satisfaction
Happiness
Lust
Pleasure
To live

'Tis only words
For you
Then let me go
Then the words foretold will flow
Let me leave this desolate place?

Then let the tales begin
For ever more to read, sustain,

I ... I ... Know your name!

Rachel Chiesly

a tortured woman
the soul remains
to fight again
for a body may be
hidden, scourged
be from the flames
the sword is forged
for only justice
retribution
reckoning
reprisal
my reward
contentment
desire
hate
pain
to die
STOP!
Wordcatcher
NO MORE!
NO!
and bare my soul
NO!

so all will know
the pain remains the same.

The prisoner!

Lady Grange

55 MILLION YEARS B.C.

Floating high above the oceans void
The peace, one piece of nothing.
An unknown silence. No sound. No birds. Silent Silence.
A stillness through all the senses
A smooth dark green ocean
Steals the eyes, glide to meet
An endless deep blue sky
Kissed love child of the mist
Water and Air unite
Concave horizon
Where the Sun rolls to dive
To entice the warm clouds caress moist whispering breeze
A rainbow arches high the bridge
The mating of the elements.
The hand of life to live.

FEAR. I shake my head to wake
I feel something awesome fathomless vibrate?

Through the silent peaceful passive calm
Comes a deep bottomless yawning rumble.
The oceans smooth flat wet virgin beauty
Begins to open like the petals of a flower
Hot molten liquid earth ejaculates
Spitting life into the mother's womb
She hisses clouds of mountains white and peach
As roaring molten lava sprays red black ash miles high
I wonder through my panic, fear, 'Is this Hell?   Or heaven?'

As if some magnificent plutonic Titan conceived to rise
The phallic crowned head's birth be born
The circled crowned king's head rests upon the sea to wait
As if to float and breathe the mists of time
Forevermore the wisdom watching waiting for the end to return
As all who know all tell all, all, and all come and all go
While everything
We all know
Remains
O

Heersht......Heersht......Heersht
Whispering waves
Sea sands salt kiss.

I glance from left to right,
Two miles of arched tormented twisted grace
From lava's coiling wreathing pain
Kissed deeply by the oceans cool refrain.

Mullach Sgar, cleft summit to *Mullach Geal's* snow white top.
And mighty *Mullach Mor's* towering 'big summit',
Be north to east by *Glacan Mor's* big hollow.
1397ft the tallest of the stretching hills *Conachair.*
Oiseval east fell, to the west and south by *Cambir's ridge,*
Mullach Bi, pillar Summit and *Ruaival*, red hill.

Amhuinn a Ghlinne Mhoir

Meandering free lost trickling cold lava stream
So sweet the taste your lips so pure
You sing your song flowing through cascading angels harps
Too many taste your sacred lips
Return so soon for a tongue's deep secret lick
The virgin juice from Mother earth,
Intoxicated dreams for women's hearts
No man will ever be the same,
All souls will spin
And beg for more
For the nectar from the gods
Is hidden within the timeless Isle
The torture of each soul's torment
The gods mischievous smile.

Temptations snake twist wreath *Glen Bay*
To the south and east ridged *Amhuin Mhor*
Dry Burn to the Big River.
From *An Lag Bho'n Tuath*, the hollow from the north
To meet at *Village Bay*
The sea to greet
With the red blood from the earth's own
Tainted peat.

Ruaival to Oiseval

The spine of the old man's crown
The highest cliffs in Britain
Above an ageless frown.

Sea-birds like snows blizzards twirl to swirl
Frenzied multitudes of screeching chants
Granted the true freedom given birth
Into the wilderness of the natural earth.

Lazy seals watch and stare
With glass bowled eyes
Flip flopping rocks
And diving deep
To disappear
And swim
Freely
D
O
W
N
To
Rise
Bubbled
Head to peep
A child so pure
Each day to play
At the edge of time
Heaven's sanctum sublime.

Coachair
Stupendous cliffs
I swoon to rise to peak to peep
As clouds of mist through spirit drift
'I am on top of the world!'
I see the curved world's edge
From the edge of the world
So grand and majestic yet so awful, overpowering, nothing.

Sea-girt Isle

The boiling sea below a foaming surging fury
The noise from an endless army's lines of attacking waves
Encircling echoing trapped acoustic frantic waves bound sound
ROAR. Charging echo, west then bouncing north then south
No escape! From the edge of the world except to disappear
Fading echo fleeing east, return forlorn to see the sea
And tell tales of wars on secret shores.
The emerald hue, glide up from Village Bay
Rich laid carpet anchored by sea-side tide tied black houses
The skirt of *Hirta,* restless waves white foaming silk frill
The old man's cream to shave his chin
Scrape the barnacles roots dug deep down in.

The Summit Ridge

The old man's head from *Mullach Mor* to *Mullach Sgar*
Matted ancient woolly hair,
Crown rimmed Sea Pink mixed Red Fescue
White Clover, Yorkshire Fogs course residue.
Dress down his gown of Green from Summit Ridge
Bell Heather tickle tinkle Purple Moor
Pink Lousewort gems
The King's gown done
Blossom pink the Thrift on Dun.

Sway yellow gold Roseroot
The crown's own jewels
On pinnacles of carved black rock
AH! 'Tis a king for sure I see
Standing at the edge of time
Guarding the gateway to?
Some timeless endless destiny.

The creeping sun begins to sink into the sea
To make the mist to float so free
And the moon begins to climb and spy
To grin or smile or wear a frown
And the old man softly shakes his smock
Breathe deeply mist
One more day's being, being kissed.

Stacked Stacs Crowned Pinnacles
The old man's crown, time cast frozen statuettes
Dancing Meridians spinning maidens absolute vortex
Acmes summit submit to nadir earth bound slumber slump
As if Medusa's glance from passing galley
Chilled children playing idle idol icon effigy
Mirror image stone cold infinite
Sense consternation some deep dread
Monumental trophies from the dead.

Stac Soay
Creep creeps the bent old beggar woman
Wading across the narrow sound of Soay
Arched motion fixed forevermore
'Caught in the act'
Four hundred yards the Soay Sound
Who dares to face the rising mists hooded swooping clouds?
Deep darkness crashing growling waves
Push through charades own cavalcade.

Stac Biorach
Pointed Stac 240 ft the most difficult Stac to climb
Fearful test of a life line quest
The challenge for a wife to gain
For a man shall prove his courage and dexterity
For death's own claim will bear no blame.

Stac Dona
87 ft, Named Bad Stac for the birds' nests are too few.
Once a lady fair with long dark hair
Shook the carrion from her dress of blue.
And within one deep dark winters night
When the Sound of Soay wailed and howled
Weeping death's own last lament
Stac Dona spun dancing upon the waves
As she sang without relent.
She twisted whirled and twirled and spun
In a tornado made from the oceans depths
And her beauty was stolen by the stars
To twinkle for eternity
As a coral's diamond cleft.

Stac Am Plastair
Stalking creature slain with time
Set moody mould
The Rascal at the 'Place of Splashing'
Some cat caught the fishy mouse
So still, not seen, pass by,
And one day safe to carry on the hunt
'NO! Dinnae float yer boat too close'
The cat's paw claw *'meeow'*
All gone forever now.

Stac an Armin
The warriors Stac 644 ft
Like a mighty breast from mother earth
Where white milk drips the pointed peak's nipple
And flow's the curve to suckle sea
One thousand Gannets
Holocaust
The milk fly flow dive free
Drips dropping white into the sea
Feeding the Titans from the Gods
The fathomless mystery.

Large and round I spin surround
This spiral path towards some truth
80 Cleitean, three Houses and stone Pyramids
Some lost souls ambling endless youth.

Envy you, I. As you sit to rest at the edge of the world
Looking o'er the arched concave
So still, alone what was your name?
Who suckle from Mother Nature?
Whilst the world succumb
Too greedy grab claw
Devouring itself
Hysterically
Turning
Inside
Out
To
O

Stack Lee
Dark Blue Monolith 564ft
I stare transfixed in wonders awe
Some rotting giant Fanged toothed skull's tooth
From a Titans battles, defeated Cracken
Or, a giant jaw waiting for some restless sleepy drifting ship
YOU?
SNAP! Secrets stolen swallowed sink the oceans belly rumble
Return and wait, pause, one thousand years
One second for the rock of ages.
Patience. The curious one will greet the gate
And what? Beyond the last mistake?

Boreray
I float south-west
I see the lion waiting to pounce or pray, to prey
I gasp bewildered
From the magnificence of Boreray.

North Isle, North land, stand grand,
Island of the 'Fortified Place'
1259ft high, towering turrets
West facing cliffs,
What warrior could defeat this resting beast?
And who would charge
To wake and meet the feast.

100,000 pairs of Puffins
Burrowed deep into the steep south-western slopes
Swirl and twirl with beaks full of dangling silver sand-eels
I wonder where and who paints the beautiful coloured beaks?
To count and watch thousands racing around a track
To rush one way quickly, NOW! Rush back.
Then dive into the wet washed surf
Swim like a fish to catch
The silver wreathing
Dangling threads
For the chicks
To feed their
Tiny beaks
& Heads.

Deep Down Boreray
The cave was carved by a giant's hand
The arched ceiling twenty metres from the sea
An empty echo chamber for whoever will, will be.
I sat within the deep carved cairn
As water dripped from ceiling high
Each splash a note an escapade
As if a sonic amplified bell
Ring rang plip plop
Surrounding
Stereo
I
Whistle
AH! Sounds
Of 1000 restless
Spirits spinning trapped
A solitary Grey Atlantic Seal
Looks left then right then straight
At me, I swoop at him and whistle loud
As the poor beast flaps splashing puddles
To escape some ghostly fate, I chase 'OOOOOO'
The poor creature squeals as a seal's melees
To dive into the endless sea's green waves
I laugh aloud and the cave laughs back
The haunting sound surround of
Spirits spinning trapped
Of 1000 restless
AH! Sounds
Whistle
I
For
Boreray, the island's island far away
Where houses nest from some soul's quest
Standing upon the wild cat's arching spine
Survey, a *HERO* to stand so proud
On top of the world
King Boreray
To rule for
Just one
Day.

Soay

Sheep Island shadowed by the Cambir
Where the Viking Callum flocked his sheep.

Soay
Soay Green
Soay Green Emerald Isle
Soay Green Emerald Isle Tiara
Soay Green Emerald Isle Tiara Crown
Soay Green Emerald Isle Tiara Crowned Jewel
Soay Green Emerald Isle Tiara Crown
Soay Green Emerald Isle Tiara
Soay Green Emerald Isle
Soay Green
Soay

The Tunnel

Standing where the seas collide
In a secret tunnel at the edge of time
Light stalks creeping living shadows
Who climb steep walls duck cracks to crevice
Look left then right bright light
I sit upon a rock within a womb
Lest fear be birth arrive too soon.

The sea storm left and the sea storm right
A rush to find itself, some waters loss return secure p
Crashing foaming white frothed fit   a
Roaring raging wars of bliss   n
Tales from an everlasting crypt   i
The secret anger's wish.   c

Eastern mouth framed tunnel vision
Boreray's beautiful green skull capped dotted sheep
OOH! A Great Auk dives through tunnelled cave
And screams '*HIORT—HIORT*'
'Remember to write my name'.

The Dùn Passage

Millions of fleeting fleeing time froze years
The waves of times licking kissing salty tongue carved rock
Divided cliffs clefts fizzy fussy fuzzy fissure rift rent spent to split
Divided chop the hand of time
Sculptured landscape stroke by stroke
Gently stride the gap's low tide.

The Dùn be Dùn
Carved Isle born
I wonder, will you float away into the sea, from the
Edge of the Earth
Discover distant epitaphs where lands grave stones
Tell tales of long lost lives
Spades dig deep for they sense your lament
Lost forlorn dour wanderer
Ferry to Valhalla
Or! Or!
Sheep may graze upon your patted slope
Chomp chew gnaw pure simple pleasure masticate
Or! Or!
Your fallen castle walls rebuilt
For warriors wars
To defend their Gods
As blood drains through
Your earth bound soil
Drank by the sea
With end
 le
  ss....
   ....
    ....

Let Dùn be Dùn
Watching from the edge of time
No need to wonder or to wander
Within time, all of time will come.

3000 YEARS B.C.

Standing still, within one day of ageless time
The edge of the world? Now flat?
For the mind twists through the past to wonder
Was our first belief our last?

Pinnacles, meridian vertex apex,
Stroke poke flicking teasing clouds
Who simply try to dance by day
AH! Now I know!
Who stirred the Milky-Way.

Foreboding aching shadows arching creeping shades.
Some wasteland cast aside
Thrown hewn forgotten
The Gods mistake now forsaken hide.

Volcanic molten moulds,
Mother earth, birth,
Spew spawn hot hatch create,
Two liquids, lava, sea, to mate
The spitting steam debate.
For hand in hand, through endless time
Dashed loves first last mistake.

Melancholy, dejection, gloom,
Left lost frozen locked
This place chills the bones, the spirit shiver
And yet the beauty haunts hunts quiver
For within the deep black rock
The diamond waits forever
Forever to be unlocked.

Breathe deep my friend
For where we go, may have no end,
I have no choice!
Hold my hand? Will you?
Upon the land of whispers at the edge of time
One place for the chosen few.

Swift swooping towers from fairytales
All one, the isles above the rising sea,
As mist and rain beats endlessly
To sink a last refrain
As if the sea desires to hide
Some swallowed sunken blame.

Beaten gabbros iron cold
Upon the Cambir and the Dùn
Black streaking lines
Tell tales of old past times,
AH! Look! See the tired aged waiting face
With crevices deep staring eyes
And tears flow through the bracken lips
And all seems all so free
Where the pale blue sky
Meets the deep green sea,

Rich jewels from silica,
The feldspar and the quartz
Cream, pink and white,
Treasures from
The star-speckled granite of the night.

Hills precipices lost in clouds
Where sea birds whirl
Like snowflakes playing,
Dancing upon a whistling wind
While all the while
Echoes repeat each screeching scream
To chill the soul
With haunting cries
'Tis what you see
Believe!
For here there
Lie no lies.

Infant infinite infantile fertile
Abandoned lost bereft
Towering
Aching crag crannies cleft.

Forgotten left forlorn
Horror beauty
Pleasure scorn.

A vibration from an energy
Expectation of all, and yet nothing remains
Some hideaway, secret,
Remnants ruminants from creations
Last remaining thunderbolt,
Intrepid luring haunting doubtless doubt
Curiosity cannot resist,
To live without the need to know, exist,
For to climb up to the mountain's peak
To find an answer to nothing
Standing with euphoria
To be a god
For just
One
Day and
Wrestle with
The earth-bound
Rock, elixirs left challenge
Phallic precipice to rise to mate
To meet the gods
A bird flying across the seas through raging storms
To land upon one solitary chosen stone
Contentment
Far, far away
Or
A home from home.
Boreray.

Heersht......Heersht......Heersht
Whispering waves, stroking, caressing,
Voices, and within one voice each word one tale,
To tell, tell tales my lot,
Sleepless nights spent tales to tell
To rise at dawn
The ink nib pen the quill to quell.

The beach was beautiful and free, with soft white sand dressed with pink and brown golden lazy waiting shells. Children in a circle poked at a giant crab with sticks of wood. Their laughter floated as an echo between turrets of spiky tortured twisting rock, as if to search for somewhere beyond nowhere, yet only nowhere was the laughter of the children to be swallowed. The sea was crystal clear yet shimmered green in the distance to form an arching concave line to meet the sky-blue sky. The sun was hot and burning. The skin of the children was dark brown. They played and splashed in the sea, their naked bodies free and natural, at one with nature. About twenty children, of different ages, climbed onto a giant floating tree, which had most likely travelled from some distant land to find resurrection through the joy and happiness of these tiny angels. The children used the tree's branch stumps to pull themselves onto the trunk and then dived or jumped into the sea with cries of joy. Boys wrestled with each other until the last remaining conqueror held his hands to the sky as he screamed a screeching cry of victory. His long haunting chilling screech bounced like a stone around the island's towering pinnacles to eventually be devoured by thousands of soaring seagulls and to then be echoed, through flying hunting beaks until the end of the end of all of time.

Back from the creeping waves were many caves where people were sitting, talking and working. The people seemed happy. They seemed very relaxed with each other and laughed freely. There was a peaceful, calm, relaxed air surrounding the people. They appeared to move slowly, without haste, as if there was no anxiety or need to rush. It was like watching a film in slow motion. There were no clocks, only the lazy sun slowly rising to return to the sea in a circle of patient time. The moon watched the sun and smiled at the earth. I was confused and deeply moved by the kind, calm, caring, peaceful, restful ways of these people. Was this utopia? No cars, trains or planes. No rushing to work, to home. No greed to grab some more of what all have. No need to chase tomorrow, to eventually find life's circle complete with a lifetimes time wasted yesterday, after an eternity spent chasing tomorrows dreams which are never fulfilled. As the dog chases its tail and once caught and bitten, wonders why the zero is the number of the fool.

I was standing within the moment. This was a place, with feelings I had never experienced before. There was peace. I could feel energy deep within myself, tranquillity, like the calm of the ocean, deep and peaceful. Within the moment was the joy of life, no need to need; only to be ... I ... I ... began to wake from sleep. I could hear my wife Annette's voice speaking in the distance, *"Colin ... Colin ... What is wrong with you, why are you crying?"*

I tried to shout to Annette, *"I have found a peace and calm, it's like ... it's like ... heaven".* I was half asleep. As I began to wake and return home I faintly heard a familiar voice, *"Well! It was far from heaven for me, for me it was hell on earth!"* 'Twas the echo from Lady Grange, I was returning to earth to meet with anxiety.

Heersht ... Heersht ... Heersht

The restless waves whisper as each moment exists to bathe away all stress. Each breath of life is like the first, and seems to last for ever. I had returned to the land of peace. I stare toward the towering pinnacles of dark contorted rock. They look like bars, bars to keep the world away and the island's secrets safe.

	A PRISON
Go away	*NO!*
Please	*NO!*
Leave	*Never!*
Me	*and you!*
With	*a quill*
Peace	*to write*

"Please! ... leave me alone Lady Grange, you are spoiling my work, you are spoiling my dream."

"Your dream will become my nightmare Wordcatcher. I am waiting for you, for the night will follow the day and winter will share the moments with the bright sunshine, for the rainbow can only exist within the moment of the storm."

Daunting caves agape, open mouthed like traps with tunnelled throats stretching into the bowels of *Hirta*. I glance to the stacs, Look! A mountainous beast with hungry bowels? Or, a mother's caring, caressing womb? A fresh water stream splashes into a large pool surrounded by small 'three foot high' walls constructed from boulders. The pool is full of crystal clear water which escapes, overflowing through a gap at the top of the reservoir to rush to merge with the waiting waves of the ocean. Six circular stone-walled buildings sit like domed shields a few hundred metres from the shore. The buildings are above sea level and the inside is dug out into the ground to a depth of one metre. The stone walls are another metre in height and from the top of the walls a concave roof spans like an umbrella supported by wooden stakes which are arched to support a waterproof layer of what looks like peat. The houses are joined by narrow tunnels. Like the houses, the tunnels are sunken below ground level and their roofs are supported by stone walls.

Inside the homes, stone furniture adorns the circular walls, the seats being covered by soft black sheepskin. In the centre of each house is a small circle of black burnt stones and resting upon the stones is some kind of 'pot-boiler' which, I presume, is for the purpose of cooking. Inside one of the pot bowls rests a spoon made from bone. I notice crude grooved pottery in most of the houses. The simple goblets are without glaze and their colour is of the earth. I can see a large jug which I am sure, from its smell, contains beer. I am bemused, *beer?* 3000 years B.C. I lick my lips and watch disappointedly as my hand passes through the jug of ale. At the rear of the houses are stone enclosures which house a variety of different animals including cattle, sheep, and pigs. I watch as men and women farm the land. A large cow is tethered to a plough which seems to be made from a wooden shaft, the end of which is attached to a thin black stone blade. As the plough is dragged through the rocky earth, two women follow, backs bent to break, as they poke some sort of crop into the awaiting furrows. The farmers are happy, singing and laughing, as they calmly take pleasure from the earth.

I can hear a woman's beautiful voice singing like an angel. I move towards the sound which floats upon the breeze like sweet perfume. I enter a house and sit to stare and bathe in the beauty of the woman's songs.

BEAUTY AND THE BEAST

Floating notes like angel-drops
Riding upon a summer's drifting breeze
Teasing ears serene
Like sweet perfume
Enchantment, chase the eternal dream.

Cascading tinkling waterfall
The hidden harp
The notes to catch a stalwart heart
The eyes bite tight
As the ears unfold
The breath of life, lost now, foretold.

In a sunken room at the edge of time
A mother sang a lullaby
Her child was laid in a wooden crib
Sleepy eyes contentment, sigh.

A child upon a fleece as white as snow
The angels flutter flying to and fro,
'Tis heaven at the edge of time
Where fingers stroke the sky
With shadows cast
Each day to pass
Time trapped in
An endless
Circle's
Line
A
Mother
Sings and
Sows a purple
Fleece, as soft as
Love lips kiss to velvet
Peach, pure joy and happiness
A child to smile as laughter spirals
Through the daunting cold stone rocks
A diamond free held in a molten hand's caress
To sparkle light from a starlit prism twinkling bright.

Her hair was black
My eyes search deep dark mountain clefts
Waves of the night
On an endless flight
Flowing float
Comb the oceans depths.

Her eyes were brown
My eyes search deep dark endless wells
The wisdom of love
The soul at rest
Breathe free
Drink from life's own chalice.

Her voice was sweet
My eyes close tight, to trap lost tears
From the wells
And the clefts
Of the future's endless pain
Close my eyes, wish, to start again.

There was a purple fleece laid at her feet
As she sowed and sang of love
With a needle of bone
And a stone to hone
Twisted wool from a wool-staff stead.

Beauty hidden within the beast
Rainbow crystals wait in tiny caves
Like painted dreams own treasure chest
Red, green, amber, brown and gold,
The molten lavas jewels at rest.

Some safe haven
No ones land
Stretching rock fingers aching weaving pinnacles
Stroking angelic songs sing ringing echoes
Kissed, soaked loving balm
To caress the giant's hand, waving east,
Steadfast all powers, persistent calm.
The beauty and the beast.

THE GALLEY

The people of Kilda were standing along the beach and staring out to sea with silent anticipation. I watched in amazement and did not know what to expect. The sea was calm and the playful mists danced as they climbed around *Stac Lee*. Suddenly, children began to scream with joy, approaching through the swirling haze of the mists was a sailboat which slid onto the shore. The galley was about ten metres in length and three metres wide. There was one tall sail made from many small patches sewn together. The wood of the boat was crude and rough, yet obviously effective. The crew from the galley consisted of five men and two women. The crew jumped ashore to receive a welcome with open arms from the islanders. There was instant chaos as everyone jumped and danced for joy.

The crew were escorted to a large cave by the beach where they sat to talk and to tell of the news from lands afar. A feast was laid upon a long table carved from a tall tree which had, at one time, floated through the oceans storms and waves to eventually drift, as other wood had done, to arrive at the edge of the world. The guests were seated at the table with about forty Kildans, while the remaining twenty islanders sat with eager ears listening to every word spoken at the table. There was an abundance of food placed on the table; lobsters, crabs, large boiled eggs, a variety of different fish and several different plates of meat. Sea-weed accompanied the meat and fish, and the crew from the galley provided drinks which they squeezed from a goat's bladder bag. The sweet smell from the liquid that the adults were drinking had an aroma like the drink I had previously seen in one of the houses.

After the food had been eaten, the boat's crew spilled two large bags of fruit onto the table. There were apples and pears, and small bags of chestnuts which the children rushed to grab, to quickly place into the hot ashes of a smouldering fire to roast. The adults laughed as the children tried to take the sweet chestnuts from there burnt black shells.

Soon everyone was fed and content and all settled to listened in silence to the teachings of one of the galley's crew. A wooden frame was placed against a wall of the cave that held a taught white animal skin. The teacher held a stick of burnt wood, *charcoal,* with which he sketched diagrams onto the taught parchment.

A picture of a potters-wheel was sketched as he told his students how the clay was turned and shaped, to then be baked in a kiln. Wheels were sketched and shown fixed to axles lubricated with animal fat. Last, yet by no means least, another parchment frame was hung onto the wall of the cave. The illustration seemed to be a kind of calendar. The writing on the parchment looked like Hebrew and was divided into twelve sections each of which was marked with numbers and pictures of the sun and moon.

After several hours the islanders carried wooden boxes and animal skin bags down to the resting galley. There were many folded black sheepskins loaded, while twice as many white sheepskins were off- loaded. From the latter I assumed the black wool to be more valuable than the white. There were many animal bladders of liquid handed to the islanders which were accompanied by sly chuckles; I presumed the content to be beer. Three tiny piglets were handed to the children who jumped for joy as they welcomed and hugged the pink squealing newcomers to the island. The last items to leave the galley were several long trunks of wood which were eagerly carried safely to shore.

The Kildans carried long flat boxes to the galley which contained jewellery made from sea shells and lava crystals. The different coloured crystals gleamed brightly as they reflected the sun's rays of brilliant light. The galley's crew was fascinated by the stones which seemed to be of great value. The last boxes I saw being loaded onto the boat were full of bird feathers which had large birds eggs placed safely inside.

Several people stared intently at the sky as they pointed and seemed to be making a decision as to the weather being favourable for sailing. Soon, the vessel was loaded and ready to set sail. The people once again hugged each other and said farewell. The crew climbed into the galley as islanders levered the hull with long wooden poles back into the waving waves.

The galley slowly became a tiny dot on the horizon which was suddenly swallowed by the late evenings setting sun.

I awoke to write and as I wrote about what I had seen, I could not but help feeling sad, as the same question returned to my thoughts over and over again.

Why did things have to change?

THE AMAZON HOUSE and the AMAZON QUEEN

Wordcatcher	**Lady Grange**
	Hello Wordcatcher!
Lady Grange?	Yes
Go away!	Now?
YES	NO
Please	Why?
You are disturbed	Restless
Restless	spirit
I only watch and listen	to tell tales
To what I see or hear	so listen to me
You listen to me	YES!
I miss the past	the beginning
Such peace	only on this island
My mind screams	AHHH! Peace
Why? Why? Why?	The nature of the species
To...To...To destroy	to destroy itself
Wars, Torture, Abuse	welcome back Wordcatcher
Go Away	Truth will always return.
PLEASE e	NO o
e	o
e e	o o

Heersht......Heersht......Heersht
Waves gently caressing sands salt kiss
Waiting at the edge of time
Peace, tranquillity, within one moment, forever

The surface of the sea was like glass and reflected the moon whose smiling face seemed to quiver upon the skin of the ocean. I lifted my eyes towards the moon floating in the sea of space amongst the dust of the stars, and his look was of sadness. I wondered which moon was a reflection and who was to mirror who in a world where opposites exist combined.

The moonlight was shining like a carpet of silver towards the horizon and the rest of the world. It was like a pathway leading from the island, or to the island. The shadows from the pinnacles of the mountainous stacks reached out like clawing fingers resting on the surface of the sea, like a mighty hand hiding to grab any lost wandering anything.

The Amazon galley floated gracefully down the glimmering pathway of the moon. Twenty long oars gently kissed the top of the ocean, as if it was important not to wake some silent sleeping giant hiding beneath the blanket of the oceans fathomless depths. Small spinning whirlpools were left behind on each side of the galley as the oars were lifted dripping drops to almost silent plops. The long galley slid to shore like a hissing serpent ready to strike.

There were a total of twenty-one Amazon women, and one stood out from the rest. She was the Amazon Queen Sgàthach from Dunscaith castle on the Isle of Skye. The Queen removed her weapons and walked towards a large round house. Inside the Amazon house the stone walls and floor were covered in thick white fluffy sheepskins. Sgàthach removed her leather shoes and walked towards the centre of the room where a long raised table stood which was covered by a golden fleece. The Queen lifted herself onto the raised table and lay down as she closed her eyes to sleep.

Beyond the Amazon house were several other similar buildings which were smaller. Into the other houses the remaining Amazon warriors lay down to rest amongst black sheepskins laid upon the floor. It was late and the weary warriors slept deeply while the moon frowned through reflections of the island's fingers resting on the surface of the sea; fingers that were now clenched into a fist as if to snatch the sleeping Amazon galley from its shore, like an irritating flea.

At the breaking of the dawn and the rising of the sun, several of the Amazon warriors entered the Queen's house where they removed their shoes, to stand waiting with bowed heads. Sgàthach spoke to the four waiting warriors, *"Come forth"*. The four warrior women quickly moved to their Queen standing two to each side of her bed. They quickly removed her clothes to bathe her body in some kind of sweet perfumed oil. Soon the Queen was dressed and standing upon the beach of *Hirta*. She shouted orders to her waiting warrior women, *"You will go back to Dunscaith and you will return for me on the first calm tide after two days have past"*. The warriors had visited the island at the edge of the world many times with their Queen and were aware that she had a need to be alone and contemplate amongst the sacred peace of the island.

As the galley raised her sail to trap a restless breeze and lazily creep home towards Skye, Sgàthach climbed to the top of Stac an Armin where she sat cross-legged and patiently waited. Weapons were not used on the sacred island as it was perceived as an abode of the Gods and yet two of the world's most skilled and powerful warriors were about to meet. The hate with which these two warriors felt for each the other was as never before known, for they had both loved, hated and lost the heart of Cuchulainn, 'The Hound of Ulster' and the hero of the 'Red Branch'. Aoife, from Alban would soon arrive to meet with Sgàthach and then, the bowels of the earth would tremble from their anger and the Gods will know their creation.

Aoife arrived in her galley late afternoon. She waved her boat and crew away and stood upon the beach unarmed. Sgàthach dived from the mountain stack into the deep blue ocean to shoot like an arrow underneath the water with the power from the height of her dive. The Queen rose from the seas waves like a Goddess to meet with Aoife. The two warrior women stood facing each the other. They stared deeply into each others eyes, as if to search for some answer or weakness.

I knew these two warrior women from my tales of the 'winged isle'. The two were masters and teachers of the marshal-arts. I had watched many times as they fought many men, often with no other weapon than the leather gauntlets which were worn on the forearms to deflect blows from hissing swords. When they fought, it was as if they danced and their beauty was held in awe by all men and women. Both women stood tall in the hot sun's rays. They wore little clothes, as the way these warriors fought was delicate and smooth like the wreathing serpent or wild cat. Sgàthach had black hair tied back which was as dark as the deepest night. Her eyes were sparkling emerald green and once stared into, it was hard to glance away. Her skin was dark brown and as smooth as velvet, flowing over her long lean muscular body.

Aoife was fair, her skin was as white as snow and her hair was yellow-gold, like the floating clouds from a golden dawn. Her body was as beautiful as her rival Sgàthach and yet some small scars could be seen on her skin. I believed these cuts to be from the fight she had with Cuchulainn.

(Ref– Poetic Tales from the Isle of Skye)

Sgàthach   *and*   **Aoife**

Your scars, your mistakes	Why have you summoned me?
I need answers	and I have questions
I have brought you here	where weapons are forbidden
To the sacred Isle	or your blood would flow
To stay my hand	I am your enemy
It takes ten times more energy	to deal with an enemy
Than	a friend
I hate you	it is good to know who hates you
And it is good to be hated	by the right people
You Harlot	you coward

Each of the women placed a hand around the throat of the other. Blood trickled down their necks from the sting of their sharp nails. Their faces were only inches apart as they shouted, spitting venom.

I sent Cuchulainn to you to die   you coward
    At your hand   without the courage of your own convictions
And you made love, Harlot   he raped me you snake
    AH! A lying whore   I will kill you! Now!
    You already have   and you have ripped my soul into pieces
Why did you not kill him   I fought for many hour's
gae bulga! The magic spear   I could not reach the spear
And you made love with him   He raped me, when I was weak
You bore his son?   Yes he stabbed me with Life instead of Death
    You whore   NO! 'Twas your mistake coward
    I will kill you   And I will leave you to live an everlasting death
NO! You will die forever   dig your nails in deep bitch
And you, wild cat I will taste the blood of your everlasting tears
You destroyed Cuchulainn   and his son Conlaoch
And also your son   he stole my womb
AH! Cuchulainn left you   I hated him
You loved to hate   I hated to love
You sent Conlaoch   to kill his Father
And neither knew   who was the other
'Til it was   too late
You could not lose   'twas my revenge, so sweet
The beautiful rose with thorn   poison forever
    You could not love   And you, Queen, could not command love

You have a heart of stone	And you think the knife will force love
You killed your love	the love you sent to me to die
The seed from your rape	was returned to avenge
A life for a life	and death to death
I hate your breath	I hate your…………

The two warriors shouted into each others faces as spit spat from their screaming mouths, while all the while their hate drew their faces closer and closer, until, for one moment of time their hate brought their lips together as their tongues thrust deeply, as stabbing knives of lust into each others mouths.

And so it was that the two women fell onto their knees to cry tears of salt into the sands of *Hirta*, from the pain of the riddle of the power of love and hate. The two warriors returned to their lands across the sea to forever wonder how the pain of life and death could be as one. As the moon and the sun may rest together in the same day's sky and the darkness of the night may hold the light of the stars; how love and hate could be so close as to share one moment of everlasting ecstasy.

Heersht……Heersht……Heersht
The sea salt sands tears
Wash away reflections, the taste soak deep,
Lips to meet the mirrored face
To taste the fruit
The lemon or the peach
For Eve to know, the sweetest juice
Is the taste so rare to reach?

THE SINKING OF THE CROWN

Generations pass
Memories last
Blades of grass
Waves flow the field sowed green
Mother's seasons bathe
Secret seeds unseen
Daises white floating firefly fairies
Drifting words caught in a dream.

Sea rise creep o'er the earth bound shore
From years tired tears cried sinking sunk
As bubbles rise from gasping caves
As if to drown the old man's head
May death redeem the dead.

The old man's eyes peep from the sea
With earth brown cracked and crannied skull
The haunting empty black-hole caves
Who dare to enter in?
May then be lost forever more.
Void. Eternal. Requiem.

Flowing sea-weed beard
Squeezed barnacle spots
Ooze white urchin
As crabs crawl pose
To pick nip nose
Tears from streams ebb filling sea
To rise to raise the flag which stays
For a crown too tall to drown
Remains the same
Forever more
The last stand
Pointing
Awe.

From Gleann Mór to Village Bay

The gentle islanders move from the drowning land at
Gleann Mór to the sheltered boat-shaped homes of An Lag
They live for love, as one for all
Any one could all recall.

Their kindness blessed
Through stormy seas
Be a light to catch an east blown wind
The fish-net sieve from the edge of time
Saved sailors bright the golden ring.

Mighty Vikings, Amazons, Celts and all
Bless the life-line from their Gods
As sailors spewed deaths sea-weed juice
Gasp swallow leap the jaws snap reap
So cool one suck of air born life
See! An angel's face, heaven, Valhalla,
Nursed child
The experience requite
Paradise
Deficit of life.

Superstitious times of doubt
Boats, Galleys, Ships dock seeking luck, or to free a curse
Sense something?
Ominous, good or bad?
To be respected
For the hands of the Gods may stir the seas ship as a leaf
Or stroke a palm to flatten restless oceans dreams.

No written laws or rules
A belief in something called nothing but love
For the island is nothing yet everything
Yet will always be itself.

Many came and many left
And all stared deep with open eyes
Souls searching for what all could feel
On the crowned rocks
Hidden paradise.

HIORT
The Earth-House 'House of Fairies' Tigh an t'sithiche.
500 B.C.—600 A.D.

Heersht......Heersht......Heersht
Waves stroking sands salt kiss
Peace and tranquillity
I listen as I sink and spin
Hundreds of voices yet every individual word, clear.
I hear a pleasant tinkling sound
Children's laughter squeals of play
I follow sounds of joy
Across this land so far away.
Fifty Fairies danced
'The dance of the five circles'

◻
◻ ◻ ◻
◻

And they turned one each the other way
As each circle spun opposite around
Each fairy did pirouette
And as they twirled and laughed and spun
My heart bereft regret.

Music played from tiny harps
Twang—Twang—Twung—Twong—Twing—Twing
The angelic strings from a golden fleece
I thought, may be from Greece.

And a whistling quartet
Blew pursed lipped horns
Spiral whispering winds
For the stacs to sway on a sunny day
Be the angels' hearts to sing
I laughed aloud and my feet did tap
'Twas the magic fairy ring.

We danced round left and we danced round right
Until the moon rose to the stars
And beams of light glowed with delight
'Twas laughter through a deep dark night.

The fairies kissed and hugged and loved
As they waved to say 'Farewell'
They all blew stardust from their palms
Towards a 'wishing-well'.

They lived in tunnels beneath the ground
Fireflies beam a rainbow glow
And through the tunnel was a room
Where a granny sat to sow.

She told secret tales from the edge of time
Of love and loss and greed and lust
Of all the wishes born from love
And the evil people cussed.

I told her of the
'Fairy—dance'
And the fairy Flag from Skye
She smiled and laughed
And shook her head
For to whisper with a sigh.

I told her of the
'Fairy—Bridge'
And a love which had to die
And she sat so sad
And bowed her head
As a tear fell from her eye.

I bade farewell
She kissed my cheek
And she wished my journey safe
With sadness in my heart to go
I left somewhere to wait.

Float from the Isle
Dip the moon swoon low
For a starlight path to glow
As a silver road, bridge a golden fold
Where the fairies tales are told.

Calum Mor's House. 600 A.D.

From enormous stones weighing half a ton
Giant Calum built his house
And no person knew from where he came
For his words were few
And he only spoke his name.

Some Viking from a distant shore
With body scars and cuts to burn
No islander would ever ask
Some things best not to learn.

He climbed the stacs
And he ploughed the fields
And he plucked the wool from sheep
But he never smiled or spoke a word
Yet alone I saw him weep.

The night was dark
And the moon shone bright
Shooting stars skipped the 'milky-way'
In a domed home-stead
In the land of dread
Giant Calum bowed his head.

Sad silent tears fell onto earth
And I wonder why the giant cry
Be love or loss or pain or hate
Or a dream's wish forlorn wait.

And as he sobbed, sat all alone
I heard a fairy sigh
But he would not look to smile with love
So the fairy floated by.

Always there to lend a hand
Many lives did Calum save
For to lift a rock, or be turn a boat
Calum, solemn,
Digging a long lost grave.

Yet at night alone, Calum would sit sad sob
And I wondered what could hurt his heart
To cry and hide his tears of pain
No words release refrain
As if some secret
Silence hide
One sob
Or tear
Pure
P
A
I
N
Pure
Tear or
Sob one
Hide silence
As if some guilt
No words secrets reveal
To hide and cry see the devil's eye
To watch pain's tears past cry.

When Calum died
The village cried
And he had built a boat
For his soul to sail
To God or Gods be heaven or hell
For a one-way ferry
Toll the death-watch bell.

Laid upon peat grass
Of the softest matt
His soul was pushed to sea
And the wind filled sail pulled to no avail
For what to be would be.

And as he sailed to a distant shore
For from his eye one tear-drop cry
For what?   I did not know........
I wish to believe him happy now
At peace where the flowers grow.

The Bee-hive Annexe

West of Tobar Childa ten domed houses stand
Like eggs laid on a field of grass
Tiny crowns sit the peat-moss cap.

With a doorway's gaping open mouthed
And a dug out tunnelled gap
Leading to a
Bee-hive
Annexe
Walls built from rough granite.

Stones carried from pro-talus ridge
Shadowed by the mighty Conachair
Ceilings built from granite slabs
With a peat-bog hairy cap skulled lid
Like little bee-hives
For families within to live.

Creep low through tunnel, wriggling worm to earth
Into an igloo nest, rest cosy warm
As the wind beyond howls
Beating walls rigid stones
At the edge of time you trespass
Lying peacefully sleeping
Taunting nature's raw claw grasp to clasp
Some vulnerable reckless shieling flange
Lightning strike and thunder roar
At the edge of time's own secret war.

Ten plots of land with tiny homes to stead
At day-break the still mist silent creep
O'er laid, raging beast now sleep
From Mother Nature's beating heart
The old man blows toward the busy world
Some itchy spots upon his scalp
Yet each and every dawn be the first day gold to red
For whatever be, will be
He will always raise his head.

Heersht...... Heersht...... Heersht

Who? May need to wish to remain to understand
Once understood
Is to remain,   or another need to wish?
For all in
All Remains the Same

The Monks did come and the monks did leave
And the Viking warriors made a stand
Yet who the need to prey or fight
Within a place
All void of
Greed.

The islanders watched as people came
Each galley with a different tale
Some speak of war and hate and death
While another of God's open door.

So many Gods to give one soul
And the wrong Gods live in hell
BAH! Tis all to one, the devils hand
Be a coin in a wishing well.

So all know all and all must know
As the old man watch, so wise
And he breathes the wind
And feels the sun
As the earth's blood flows inside.

And the old man smiles and wonders
Of this puzzling riddle
'What the fuss?'
As people rush-rush-rush
For a need is greed to force to ask to tell your way to sway...
Listen!!!
You may find something deep inside
From an island far away.

Heersht......Heersht......Heersht
Sleepy waves stroked brow to wake
Voices...Voices...Whispering
To sleep in peace
To whisper
Tales

I find myself standing in silence
With the whispers in the waves
I cannot understand this place
There is everything here and yet nothing
All has happened here yet nought remains
All Remains the Same
But some ugly warts of wars waiting game,
Like a ticking bomb
I wonder?
If the old man's crown be bombed by a mushroom
When time returns as nature tries to heal her cancer
Will, Will the old man's head still be
Waiting for the end of time?
Is he the end of time?
When the planet is barren
Will he watch for eternity?
And as his crown is swallowed by the ocean
Is he the one to ask the last remaining question?
WHY?

THE VIKINGS FUNERAL

The timid islanders watched
Staring out to sea
For within the night, from a deep, dark, black blanket void
A flickering flame fire wave as if to tease
The waters wet waves weave splash lick torment
As cat to mouse to play wreath, wrath, wraith, taunting death
Whilst hissing water drips spitting
As steam clouds rise from a kissing dragon's breath.

*

Dot
With intent
Gradually, slowly
Creeping tides death
Direct rudder to rebirth
Sail on to the edge of the earth
Closer and closer, islanders run to hide
Tunnels deep to meet a subterranean hive
As the mighty ghost ship sparks and crackles
Earth, Fire, Water, Air, Burning brightly Rose red flower
As the ferry sails from the depths of Hell, Knap of Howar
Be a one-way trip through Utgardr to Midgardr to the fortress
Island Boreray Valhalla, crossing the kingdom of the dead
Silver coins pay the ferry man to reach the other side
Sail free O burning ship, float the death watch ride
When the mast beam sigh, let the mainsail fly
As the ashes, smoke eternal, spiral high
With sword in hand warriors fight
To greet the cave of hollows
At the edge of the world
Where time is still
Watching with
Intent
Dot
*

Heersht......Heersht......Heersht
The long ship slid to shore
Through restless waves
By God's back door
To the land of shadows
No key to lock
At the edge of the world
Where time forgot.

Lots of tiny eyes peep, peep, peep,
And slowly creep, creep, creep,
Towards? To meet, meet, meet,
Pit pitter pat of feet, feet, feet.

Within the ashes dust to dust
In a ring of stones
By a corbelled cist
Two souls to rest
Forever kissed.

Be a long broad sword
Spear and old whetstone
Spin the blunt blade knife
For the bone to hone.

Tortoise brooches turquoise blue
With a crown to frown
In the morning dew.

Two urns of
Danish silver
Buried in a keep
Used to pay the ferry man
Be a safe soul's saviour meet.

Resting peacefully sleeping
Side by side
At the foot of *Aoismheal*
By dawn's morning mists
*Heersht......*Waves stroking bliss
Loves gentle lips first kiss.

Heersht......Heersht......Heersht
I rise from the mist of the restless waves
I lick my lips to taste the salt
Of the old man's tears.

I stand to face this place
To wake to wonder, hesitate
Some cast off Heaven? Hell?
Or simply left forgotten?
Wasted waste?
Some remnant of creation, for the earth was created?
I wonder amongst my wandering thoughts,
No, no answers!
For fools lay laws and set the rules to change what be,
The multitudes of Man made Gods dictators
And all know all the answers
For each has been granted the one divine link
When did one stand still for to listen or to think.
And when did one put down the sword
To leave at rest the peaceful gifts
So free amongst the cliffs
Where the bunkers hide to ambush enemies
AH! Some tiny place untouched
To join with war and play the game
Be a cancer on the old time face
Welcome to the Holy Human Race.
As the species, nature devours all beauty
To sit and wait for the last sunset
And through the holocaust, and after aeons
Of settling dust
The pinnacles from the crowned sphinx
Rise from the ashes
As was, Has been, and Will be, and will Return.

BAH! NO! Leave alone,
For I see a crown upon a Majesty
As old as time, or older if time passes by to miss?
Some peeping giant's peaceful head,
Why Change? And take?
Takes more, to give.

THE GHOST OF LADY GRANGE

Lady Grange	Wordcatcher
You see things! Wordcatcher!	*Things!*
Be careful what you whisper	*Go away*
Waiting whisper catchers	*Let me rest*
May hear you	*I say what I feel and see*
See seer see	*you are disturbed*
Oh Yes!	*What do you want from me?*
We are similar	*You and I?*
Yes! We both see	*Seers?*
You saw an innocent man murdered	*Yes*
And you spoke and paid	*with the years of my youth*
And I could see thousands of deaths	*for a war*
From fools who would not listen	*led by fools*
AH! The Prime Minister	*the man who hunted Dolphins*
I knew what was going to happen	*where?*
The Jacobite rebellion	*Culloden*
Yes! I could see the holocaust	*and I 'Bloody Sunday'*
I was silenced	*as was I*
Hidden away in a prison	*Yes*
So we have	*a lot in common*
Persecution	*a woman with opinions*
Political opinions	*your fate was sealed*
As was my	*years of torturing isolation*
Punishment for telling the truth	*the truth may be hated*
As fools play with thousands of peoples lives	*gambling*
I was not against the rebellion	*but you could see*
I knew our army would not be supported	*near London*
I said my peace	*and you became a threat*
Honour cannot be given	*nor stolen for it lives in the heart*
I was not afraid	*you are brave*
And I was right, thousands died	*an embarrassment*
And a woman	*suppressed yet not surpassed*
Hidden away as a criminal	*until today*
I have waited many years for your pen	*to catch the words,*
And release my guilt	*for a woman scorned*
And take the gag from my mouth	*your words will be written*
For all to know	*and your innocence*
	Proclaimed

DUN-FIR-BHOLG

Heersht......Heersht......Heersht
Within one moment of one gentle wave
No need to count
And yet so many
This....This peace....I have never known before
Such peaceful ecstasy
Remain relaxed....I begin to try, my mistake,
Too late! One moment passes by.
The old man smiles
The dark cave gaping joy
A happy tear-drop drips
The twisting trickle
Through canny cranny crags
Deep hewn the line of time
The wisdom of the wise old man
Monumental for all time.

Sweet tinkling tiny chimes from *Mullach Sgar*
Like fairies dancing dressed with bells
I float to see what be
For we all must play fate's destiny.

Dolerites Grey Blue-buff
Shimmering wet bathed naked to the sun
Quickly, catch the blanket's glistening twinkling dance
As picks pick chipping chip
The Viking bells
Praise Njörôr

AH! The pounding punching hammer's beat
Tall chimneys furnace
Weaving smoke
Waving sweet incensed
Earth born bourne peat to peak
Charcoal and iron
Steal steels battered swords of war
The chiming choir

Beat the hands of Thor.
From *Mullach Sgar* to red *Ruaival*
The flowing green gown
Down of Dun
Where mountain titans hiding peep o'er hill tops precedent
God's chiselled aching Osterveaul.

Dun-Fir-Bholg, castle of 'The men of Quivers'
Towering over Village Bay
Agape the jaws soak flowing rivers
To snap the trap
Venus venom
Raining reigning arrows fall from heaven.

Ten ships of Picts pictured face licks
Dark blue tattooed scars
Cut deep the face blood weep to weal
Fast to shore an open door
With shields held high
To catch the arrows, hissing fly,
For far above
'Skildir' the Mighty Vikings cry

Rolling rocks boulders dash to crack
Skulls and bones
The Picts scream 'Cináed to rule'
The Vikings yell 'Óôinn'
While the old time mountain tastes the blood
Which flows o'er hills the valleys hood
Through black caves mouths
To swallow deep
Into bowls hell's endless
bottomless keep.

Bloods lust food fed
To count the dead
The Picts return to sea
While the Vikings cry
We live or die
For the sword in hand is free.

HÖKUNÓTT

Mid-winter night
Dun-Fir-Bholg
Shrouded towering castle walls of Dùn
Euphoria's rapture ecstasy
Deaths crown battle won.

Fire baskets burn around the castle walls
Leap light lick stretching
Returning to a sunburst set
A bridge across the universe
To unite where time once met.

From Long Island
All stare in awe
Be Skildir's crown of Golden light
The head of Thor and war.

Families stand wrapped warm in wool
As hot red light climb's castle walls
Flames try to flail assay
Kissing stars lick the 'Milky Way'

The alter standing frozen trapped in a winters night
Carved chipped chiselled hacked hewed hewn slab
Flat grey cold monolith
Reflect Valhalla lain slain dolerite
Breach birth gap assail agape
From earth to heaven
Talons claw the pearl strewn gate
Deliberate castrate
Breath breathe death reborn, dying to live
The gods move in mysterious ways, initiated,
Begot begat begotten the spawn spurned gift, created.
People stare upwards into open space
As if to find some answer
Bolting thunder-flash
An omnipotent
Gratitude
O

O
Gratitude
An omnipotent
Bolting thunder-flash
As if to find some answer
People stare upwards into open space
Begot begat begotten the spawn spurned gift, created.
The gods move in mysterious ways, initiated,
Breath breathe death reborn, dying to live
Deliberate castrate
Talons claw the pearl strewn gate
From earth to heaven
Breach birth gap assail agape
Reflect Valhalla lain slain dolerite
Flat grey cold monolith
Carved chipped chiselled hacked hewed hewn slab
The alter standing frozen trapped in a winters night.

Adorned with ruby quartz onyx chalcedony
Pillars raise praised alters stone
Stairway to heaven's
Celestial throne.

Toasts to Óôinn
Victory and the King's success,
The sacrificial beast and beaker blessed
Be the blood and bones of a holy quest.

The Chieftain's *fulls* to
Njörôr and Freyr, for food and peace,
Sarajin and Thor for war and lust
Sumbel, jewels, drinking horns, bowls, jugs, rhenish amphorae
From Lilla Villa
Wine from the Gods Wodden, Odin.

'Ullr' all cheer
Aurora Borealis
Illuminates the canvas crape
O Northern Lights
'HOOORAR'
The Gods appear in space.

HIRTA

The Old Village 1615 *(March 7ᵗʰ)*

Lachlan Corry sat upon the rise from Gleann Mór. He pushed his back hard against the stone walls of one of the many surrounding Cleits. He chewed a piece of old dried gannet he had taken from the Cleit store and relaxed into contemplation as he watched the setting sun which slowly sank to hide behind the distant Long Island.

Lachlan was 19 years of age and on the morrow he was to become a man. His heart thumped hard against his chest as he thought of his balancing upon the tip of the Mistress Stone. One falter would result in his falling onto the jagged rocks below which were like the teeth of a beast waiting to devour any weakness. He had practised the balance which was upon one leg one thousand times and the manoeuvre was simple when standing on the ground. Luchlan prayed to the God which the holy Priest had told him of from the book of the bible. "*Please, one and only God of all Gods, keep the winds from Ruaival tomorrow and keep me from the waiting teeth of the Devil below who lives in Hell amongst the teeth of the beast. Let me live to be a man and marry Mary MacPherson from the third cottage, the one with the stags horned head hanging on the wall. If you do this for me God, I will name my children after your saints and make them pray to you and sing your praise. Now! If I fall to die all praise will be lost, so be with me God, Amen.*"

Lachlan looked to his left and then to his right as if to catch a fleeting glimpse of God. All he could see was the rising green concave of Gleann Mór, like some gigantic frozen wave with the tiny black-houses below riding the surf of the earth.

As he stared below at the cluster of twenty tiny cottages, dusk descended like a blanket of the night to reveal scattered stars like pin-pricks from a worn cascade. Luchlan watched the cottages below as warm lights slowly began to glimmer from their windows. Two cats howled at each other like some devils demons crying from hell. The haunting noise from the cats was suddenly stopped by a frantic growling, barking dog.

Silence returned to the village and darkness swamped the peaceful homes, the only noise was the occasional bray from one of the many sheep scattered over the island.

Luchlan began the short walk down Gleann Mór to his home which he shared with his mother, a widow of some twelve years. Her husband had died from a tragic fall while climbing *Stac Armin*.

As Luchlan passed the house of his betrothed, Mary, he could hear faint voices from within, for the wooden shutters of the windows were slightly open. He stood in silence, like a statue in the deep darkness. His heart was beating hard as his mind wondered, what was to be seen inside? He could feel the excitement; 'twas like the times he climbed a mighty stac; the fear of the challenge and the risk of failure. He remembered the day he had proposed to Mary and how her face turned to red as he kissed her lips for the first time. All that was left for him to do was to prove his manhood and then they could be married.

Luchlan could not resist, he moved slowly and silently toward the thin crack of light of the shuttered window. Suddenly his breath was taken away, for in the orange glow of the flame from the oil light, Mary stood naked while her mother combed her long black hair. He felt he should run and yet he was fixed to the spot for her beauty was such that he could not avert his eyes. He had never seen a woman in the state of undress before, but had listened to many tales from lustful lads with lustful thoughts. He stared at Mary's pearl-white body and the deep red pinnacles which crowned her mountainous breasts. His eyes glanced down to the darkness of a cave of life, warm and wet with hidden secrets he longed to explore. He could not believe how the curves of her waist and hips could have existed underneath the thick, crude clothes she wore each day. He had never seen such a beautiful sight in his life and now longed for the day they would be married.

Mary's mother combed her daughter's long raven hair which waved from her head down to her waist. *"Mary, my arm is aching, I think you look beautiful and Luchlan will be the luckiest boy in the world".*

"Mother! Luchlan will not be a boy after tomorrow, he will be a man".

Luchlan moved quietly from the window and started to pray as he walked home, *"Please God! Help me tomorrow and thank you God for your wonders to behold".*

The Mistress Stone

Luchlan had a restless night, with thoughts of love and lust and death, and by the dawn he arose to climb Ruaival to find the 'Well of Youth'.

The Well of Youth
The early morning's painted dreams
Strike stroke red gold orange yellow
Twist a twirl spin meet to merge
Mist white wisp wishing-well.

Climbing to some secret what?
To test the hand of God and fate
The finger or the toe default
The final revelation
God's chosen thunderbolt?

Wet rock ridge
Claw fingers tips
Slippery moss mourn the morning dew
Foggy mist, missed grip
The soul and body taught, taut, tort, twist askew
Heroes?   Fools?   The chosen few?

And to the top of
Nothing O Everything
Awaits the genius of the Fool
Sat by the fathomless pool.

"Mortal boy today you test the test
For the ferry man awaits your quest
And may not return lest paid
Grave graves grave
One coin to persuade?"

Luchlan flicks a silver coin into the
Well of youth
Eyes closed tight to wish, a wish
And the pool disappears forevermore
Fools dreams once cast dismiss.

Luchlan walked toward cone-shaped Ruaival and began to climb from the south-west base to the summit. Each finger delicately feeling for ledges to grip as each toe from naked feet follows arching instep, while craning neck and searching eyes seek the next grip of hope. One false move or slip will be the first and last mistake, for fallen angels receive no mercy. On and on, like a twisting weaving snake, moving upward and never looking back down, for now there can only be the end of the test, and victory, or endless shame, or.......Death.

Luchlan thinks of his truelove Mary and their wedding, he would prefer to die rather than live one day without her love. Suddenly Lachlan comes face to face with the Mistress Stone. He can hear the cheers from the islanders below him and waves his arm to the excited crowd. He can see his mother far below and knows the fear which will be clutching at her heart and he knows the tears will be in her eyes. He can see his truelove Mary. She is waving her arm and holds one hand over her mouth as if to stop some last cry of weakness. He can see the priest standing with open arms and looking into the sky while shouting as loudly as he can so God may hear his words, *"Bless this boy this day O God"*.

Luchlan closes his eyes and reminds God of his prayer from the previous evening, *"Please one and only God remember my prayer from last night and I still promise to make my children pray to you each day, OH! And I have paid the ferry man so please don't let him take me. Amen"*.

> Some leaning fallen stones from endless time
> Waiting at the edge of life
> The gates of death
> Arched giant
> Boulders
> Cleft
> Of
> Life
> To die
> To live again
> Rebirth through
> Dice tossed by the
> Hand of choice to gamble
> All, and be reborn, fate's ecstasy of life or death.

Luchlan mounted the Mistress Stone, as excited cheers instantly became smothered by a blanket of silence. The massive triangular boulder Luchlan was standing on looked like it had been carefully placed into position by some giant child stacking stones, for no person could have placed the 'Mistress Stone' in such a precarious position.

Luchlan walked to the edge of the Mistress Stone and his legs began to shake. He closed his eyes tightly and spoke to himself, *'Relax, there is no wind; God is with me, now, just....just do it'.* He placed one foot in front of the other, toe to heel, and then bending forward as he placed his clenched fists in front of his feet, with only his one heel remaining on the rock. He opened his eyes and all he could see was open space. He felt like he was flying and the adrenalin rushing through his body made him feel like he could fly if he wanted to. Suddenly there was a loud roar from the waiting crowd far below.

Luchlan smiled, he had become a man and was looking forward to knowing what it felt like.

Heersht......Heersht......Heersht
I feel the sunlit breeze stroking my face
Peace....fall back into sleepp
                               p
                          p
I hear happiness, laughing, so free,
I remember the beginning
The peaceful beach, slow and carefree
I feel a fluttering in my stomach
Butterflies fly riding a rainbow
I watch floating colours, bubbles
Floating around the stacs of Hirta
Peace...bliss...calm...utopia...euphoria

Sleeeeppppppppppppppppppppppppppp

Oooo!   I awake, suddenly startled
In front of me stand two men.
The Priest and the Wise Old Man!
The tension and hate between the two is pure.

The Wedding

Black wool sheepskins thrown, clouds lain bright green grass
Rest yellow flowers cast white framed purple heather
While coloured stones from sea-washed sands
Jewels, rainbow rings, sweet children's angels sing.

Food a plenty spread for all
Fish liver stuffed into wide-eyed fish-heads 'ceann-cropic'
Gannets and Fulmar roast or boiled
Smoked Puffins spread with 'giben' oil.

Boiling sea plants dulse and slake
Silver-weed roots, dock boiled and scurvy-grass
And mounds of eggs boiled, grilled and fried
Rare, rare red meat and bread
A special wedding treat.

Nettle root and barley beer
Porridge biscuits
Cream to
Smear.

Bleak black rocks brave the bashing tide
Sun scope scoop clouds affray
The isle of stacs
Stacks jewels on the crown this day.

Cnoc a Bheannaichta
On the 'Hill of Blessings'
Walked a maiden fair
All dressed in white with flowing hair,
Her smile bathed the sun
So bright for joy
I had never seen the heavens
Bow to smile so coy.
Her radiance and purity
Shone through the rocks of destiny
As if the world stopped for one day
To steal a butterfly at play.

Luchlan wore a brown leather doublet
Over a drop yoke shirt of white
A long lost gift of pant's from overseas
Of deep dark blue
Soft velvet o'er his knees.

From *Tir fó Motifs*, the otherworld
Land under waves
To the Hill of Blessings
The dark satanic crowned steeples
Bow their peaks in dread
Such wonder
From a woman's love
In awe to bow the last mans head,
For beauty and the beast rock, sea-gulls chime
In the land of doubt
At the edge of time.

The Priest and ancient wise man
Take to pose
For within the crowded mists
Be always one who stands who says he knows.

The Priest	*The Ancient Wise Man*
May God bless you both	*Upon the Hill of Blessings*
And may his love be with you	*May your love seed to grow*
For ever more eternal	*To last forever*
And the shadow of the cross	*And the climbing of the stacs*
Be your love to grow and grow	*Keep you safe from far below*

Mary: *Truly my sweetheart is now a man who will climb the tallest mountain to catch the mighty Auk.*

Luchlan: *Mary, my dear love is the maid with raven hair and beauty which shadows the sun.*

Mary: *Thou art my handsome joy, thou art my sweetheart, thou gavest me the first honied fulmar.*

Luchlan: *Thou art my turtle-dove; thou art my golden dawn,
your voice is my music to ease all ills.*

Mary: *Thou art my Hero; thou art my basking sunfish,
the puffin and the black-headed guillemot.*

Luchlan: *The mirth of my eyes and the essence of my joy thou
art and my sweet sounding lyre in the morning mist.*

As soft lips kiss
What mountain cannot but tumble
For within the crown of glory
The jewels of love's own deity
Meet stars cascade confetti.

From deep within the earth does rumble
As the universe turns inside-out
Be all who claim to know
Smile, as they try to hide a frown to crease the twist of doubt
As the towering stacs crags cracking scowl
By the moon in a deep dark night
A lone dog sits to howl
To the tune of a timeless plight.

The Wedding Dance

Dancing hop skip skipping
Happiness and peace and love
So pure, no greed,
God from above?

Each person twirls and skips and jumps
No judge to judge if a hand should slump
Or if a step to fall all spread
To dance with glee around a heather bed.

Arms link left and arms link right
As the people sing and laugh by the bright firelight
And if a note should fall or rise
No one cares
For the brides wide eyed.

Such happiness! I wish would cast
Through time and space
In an hour glass!
To show the world, which soon will sink
Through need we feed
Greed's sunken brink.

I awoke at home, at dawn, and felt a sadness
while in my heart was such a happiness
I had never before experienced
I rushed to see the sea
to try to tell the tale
of a happiness
which one day
I prayed
may
be
f
o
r
e
v
e
r

It was dawn's first light and the priest assembled the villagers, *"I have been granted a vision from the night. My vision was of a mighty wounded eagle which landed amongst a flock of lambs. The eagle sat amongst the lambs and harmed them not. Eventually the eagle became strong and took to flight to leave the lambs in peace"*

The Coll MacDonald Raid 1615 (April 15ᵗʰ)
The Outlaw Coll Ciotach (Ketoch alias Macgillespick)

From *Tigh an Fhairfaireadh* the watch-man shouts
From the Saddle below *Mullach Bi*
"Three ships .... Three warrior ships"

Young women and children run to hide
Amongst the tunnels of *Mullach Sgar*
As three ships slide to shore
With flapping sails and heaving bows
To land to rest
The 'Men O War'.

Fifty men with shields and bloody swords, torn clothes and skin cuts broken bones, jump to shore and look to left, then right to fight, but nought to see but silent towers from looming rocks foreboding calm and carefree stare.

"I am Coll McDonald from Colonsay, I wish you no harm just peace, food, and rest from the toils of war".

The warriors became silent and felt uneasy within the shadows of *Hirta*. Robert Williamson spoke in a whisper as if not to wake some sleeping giant, *"Let us set sail Captain, for this place is God forsaken and haunts my soul".*

"Be at ease man, I Macgillespick who has fought battles throughout the land will not run from the shadows of wasted rocks. Now! Kneel to pray for the Lord will abide with us.

O Lord God
Who has been by our side
At the battle of Islay
Against the evil
Sir Oliver Lambert
Guard our souls against
The beasts from the darkness.
Bless my men.

Our Father whom art in the heavens
Hallowed be thy holy name
Let thy kingdom come
And thy will be done

On earth against your evil enemies
As it is in your kingdom
Forgive me.....and my men any sins
As we forgive those who surrender after trespass
And lead us not into temptation lord
And deliver us from our evil enemies
For thine is the kingdom
The power and the glory
Amen.

Shout Amen you heathens or I will fillet you with my cutlass".
AMENNNNNNNNN

The priest from the village slowly approached the sandy beach after seeing the warriors praying to God. *"I bid you welcome sir and I pray you visit with peace for there are no weapons or people of war upon Hirta".*

"Greetings sir I bid thee well, I am Coll MacDonald and these are my brave warriors who fight in the name of the Lord God almighty, we seek food, rest and peace, nothing more will be asked and nothing more will be given, what say you sir?"

The wise old man from the village approached slowly, limping with his staff, *"I welcome you and your men Coll MacDonald, what we have is little, but will be shared amongst you and your men. Now! Come and wash in the stream and let us balm your wounds and splint your broken bones".*

In a long communal house a table was set for three. Outside the house Coll MacDonald's warriors sat upon the green grass and drank beer from goats' bladder bags. They were served dried gannets seasoned in the *cleits*, *"BAH! This tastes like a sweaty leather boot soul".*

The warriors' wounds were treated by the islanders, who were used to broken bones and cuts from the accidental falls of their climbers.

Inside the house the wise elder from *Hirta* bid his two guests to rest in their seats around a table spread with food. The table was laid and a large joint of roast venison which Coll had given as a gift for the meal sat temptingly in the centre. Crude pot mugs were placed beside each of the men and were filled with beer which Coll had also provided.

The village elder rose to his feet to propose a toast, *"I*

welcome Coll MacDonald from Islay to our humble table and may Hirta be at your service and of aid to you with your journey".

The priest stood to speak as the elder sat back into his chair, "In the name of the Father and the Holy Ghost I bless this meal and all at this table, Amen". Coll and the elder both joined in with the final, "Amen".

Coll tore a piece of tender roast venison from the joint laid on the table, "AHHH! I have waited a long time to taste such sweetly cooked meat ARRR!" He tore savagely with his teeth at the hot juicy meat, "AHHH! Fit for a king, what say you priest?"

The priest ate slowly and delicately, "The lord will provide, and I thank him for his gifts"

Coll laughed loudly, "HAAA AAA AAA, 'twas nae the Lord God provided yer meat man, it be Donald Gorm MacDonald from North Uist and it will be yer bowels he will be windin' on a pinion if he catches ye, HAAAA HAAAR HAAR".

The priest chocked as he spat the meat from his mouth, "I will not be eating stolen meat sir!"

Coll MacDonald snatched the meat from the priest's plate, "HAA HAAR, nae good a wastin' good meat man HAA HAAR."

The elder interrupted to break the tension, "Please try some eggs sir they are still warm from being boiled"

"Thank you old man, now tell me, where are all your people, I have only counted ten men and ten women. I mean them no harm for I may be known for many wrongs, but I have never killed a man who was not out to take my life and I have never loved a women who did not wish to share my bed".

The priest interrupted angrily, "Mind your tongue sir, for your drink seems to loosen your words."

Coll laughed loudly, "You sit there as a Holy Priest, are you a Catholic? Or do you blaspheme? ARR! Do you know the Lord's Prayer sir? Do you know the scriptures? HAA! I thought not. And are you aware Priest, that on March the 10th only four weeks hence, the catholic priest John Ogilvie was tortured for eight days. HA! He was tortured and hung by the neck, by order of King James VI for refusing to acknowledge the spiritual supremacy of the King above the Pope, should I take you back to Edinburgh sir? HA! Have you the courage of your convictions sir? Will you face the King and declare your loyalty to the pope, HAA?"

The priest jumped from the table and quickly left the room, as the outlaw Coll roared with laughter, *"Run priest run, for God sees all, you cannot hide, HAA HAAR HAAR".*

The elder bowed his head with embarrassment, *"Please be tolerant of the priest for I believe him to be more of a seer than a holy man, but his intentions are good".*

Coll MacDonald and **The Ancient Villager**

Coll MacDonald	The Ancient Villager
Your kindness holds me in awe	'Tis our way
For such kindness I have never known	'Tis all we know
Just wars and death	And to heal
The dead to groan	Pure simplicity
Fear, always waiting	We have fear
Anticipating death	We know the face of death
Killing, yet always another fight	As the mountains we climb
Endless wars	We must fulfil some challenge?
I...I...I am a sinner	We all sin
Mine is the worst	Hold my hand my child forget
I...I...I have taken pleasure, lust, from...	The killing
I wish to change	Changes are always possible
I need the peace with you, here	On Hirta?
I...I...Will stay here, in peace	Yes! Hirta welcomes all
No...No...I am not ready yet	And all will be
Pinnacled head of wisdom	I am only standing still
Waiting	Waiting
Timeless immortal	Nothing
You have some key	We have nothing
This place is a gateway?	Nothing is nothing
This place is holy?	Names come and they go
Your home fills me with sadness	It is no ones home
For I crave for your peace	A piece of nothing?
I will stay here!	....
I will be at peace!	....

....
....

I am too restless, I...I...Feel fear	People fear nothing
Yet there is nothing to fear	Only the unknown
I cannot let go....of...	Nothing?

'Twas the end of April 1615, and Coll MacDonald and his three ships were made ready to set sail. *"Well! My friend, old man of wisdom, I must bid ye farewell as I set sail to follow the rolling of the sun".*

The ancient old man held Coll tightly in his arms, *"May God sail with you and hold the devil at bay and remember to soon return for our hand of love and peace is always here for you"*

Coll climbed aboard his galley and roared, ***"Set sail ye heathens!*** *And I will return soon my friend and I thank you for all the food supplies".* Coll waved as flapping sails tugged towards destines fortunes of fate. Coll shouted at the top of his voice as he disappeared into the swirling mists, *"Do not forget to tell Sir Rory MacLeod of Dunvegan that the outlaw Ketoch Macgillespick thanks him for the loan of his rent HAAA HAR HAARRRRRRRRRRRRRRRRRRRRRRRRRRRRRR"*

As the three ships vanished and Coll MacDonald's voice became a whisper within the wind, the ancient old man of Hirta fell to his knees with laughter, *"HAA HAAR HAAR I cannot wait to see the steward's face when he calls for the food provisions for his rent HAA HAAR HAAAAAAAAAAARRR.........*

Friends

Two strangers at the edge of time
Sat within the crown of space
The mirror be the looking glass
To stare and watch and wait.

And all in all is all the all
For within one moment's silence
Eternal, but one debate.

You and I?
We share a time
We go nowhere
For nothing is the final line.

Some bond a hand held tight
For there will always be someone
Even within the darkest night.
LOVE

UTOPIA

Heersht...... Heersht...... Heersht

Many days spent nights
Within a peaceful bliss
Within the whisper of the waves
The breeze to sands salt kiss.

This?   Hypnotic calm
Safe?   Peaceful.

Watching sunsets blazed inferno
O'er distant lands
Racing raging clouds rush crash to meet, then dash away
As furious fiery twisting leaping lapping licking flames
Living in one battle's heavenly moment
Then? Wait? Crave for the next
Some, elixir? Drug crazed nostrum of self destruction?
War of wars world's vexed cavalcade
Marching armies wispy cloudy shapes
Passed spirits? Regret rues roles rules raid charade barricade
Life or death perambulates
Whores hordes each virgin death
Collecting, amass, a mass for   God?   King?
Until the setting of sun's sons
Black bleak seep creep. Repeat?
Turmoil o'er the distant hills
The dancing reaper reaps.

I turn to look, within the crown
The anchor of the world
The macrocosm's lost microcosmus, preserved example
The black diamond all pass by
Within the ugly pointing spars crown jewels
Nothing to fear
Hidden from all fools
Only birds and waves adhere.

A mini world of happiness, content for now,
Temptations apple's pips to core
Eyes restless waiting always wonder
Is there something more?

One people, one organism
United organized
Why destroy ones self?
When all around
The winds and seas attack.

Simplicity purity equity integrity
Greed or need?
Winters warm red crackling fire
Open mouths for food to feed
For a true need be a love to care
The hand which gives will always share
Then the mask is gone
Innocence, as a child, the soul laid bare
Life's needs, the simple eggs to share
Fresh water, breathe deep the cool freshness of the air
Where if ones needs unseen decreed
Then the hand which gives
Is void of greed.

Parliament! All meet and talk at the same time
And no one listens, universal politics,
Success, happiness,
For he who thinks he knows tells all
Then all who know then feel content
For all, know all, in all, only death relent.

A wrestles breeze surrounds my soul
As lightening strikes and thunder roars
And the oceans waves rise wash and bash
Sometimes a key lost from the past.
I hurry home for a restless change is in the air
I know I should not now be nowhere
Lest a wandering soul be lost somewhere.

ST. KILDA
The Beginning of the End

The Apostle of the North
Angus Fiddes
John Sands
Angus Fiddes
John Mackay
McDiarmid
Neil MacKenzie
Leprosy
John MacDonald
Alexander Buchan
Dean Monro
Chief MacLeod
Martin Martin
Roderick the Great

Regeneration	Utopia
We bring to you civilization	We are a civilization
We come to show you the ways of God	We pray to God
So your souls may enter heaven	We are already in heaven
We bring to you the scriptures	Thank you
You are all sinners	OH! We know No murders! No crime!
You break the Sabbath	How can we break what we do not know
You blaspheme against the Lord	We pray to God
Whose God do you pray to?	The God of peace and Love
You have no church	God is everywhere
God is nowhere	Then God is here
You can be drawn and quartered	And you cannot force devotion
Enter into the kingdom of God	Show me God's kingdom
The kingdom is within us	And we will enter, where?
We cannot see the kingdom	Then how do we know
Have faith, take my hand	But, there is blood upon your hand
What blood?	Blood from the deaths
Who's blood	From the thousands who followed you into
'Twas in God's name	War
We followed the cross	You made the cross
We defend the cross	And crucified God's son
You are bitter	We are at peace with God
You will renounce your evil ways	We have nothing to renounce
The rack will make you	Force, torture,
Acknowledge the devil within you	I know the devil in me
AH! You accept you are possessed	Only by you and yours
We will stay until you change	It has begun

You will accept the Lord God   For we do not fight
  Your houses are unclean   Yet we are content
Your houses are built incorrectly Yet we are safe and warm
  Your land is not separated   For we live as one
  You make pagan sacrifices   And you will make a sacrifice of us
  You will become as us   For now there will be no return.

The Black Prince

Heersht.... Heersht.... Heersht..

Angry waves beat beats
To pound the crowns shores rocks
Restless in my sleep
The old man roars in pain as th...

ARRRRRR

BANG.... BANG.... BANG

The islanders run in fear scuffling to hide within secret earth bourn tunnels. The passing ship *'Black Prince'* fires its guns into the stacs, whilst sailors shout and cheer in amazement as thousands of white sea birds swirl like smoky snow flakes to shade the sun.

    The scene reminds me of a snow dome, which when shaken twirls with clouds of white.

    Soon the ship's three masts of giant ghostly white sails dissolve into the horizon heading for the glory of the ways of wars.

    A long time past, the islanders returned to wonder why?

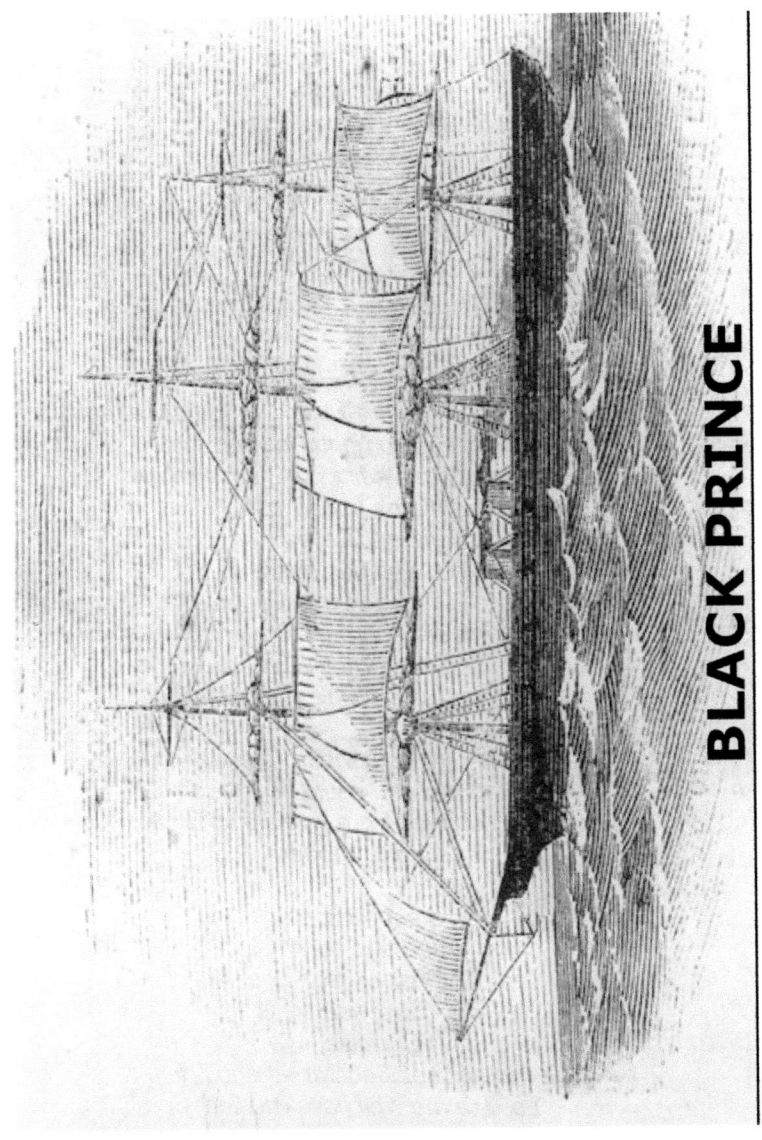
BLACK PRINCE

Heersht……Heersht……Heersht
The waves turn inside out
Spitting white frothed foam
As if having some kind of fit.
I turn to run
Yet the waves surround me
NO! NO!
They are crashing onto me
AHHHHHHHHHHH
I awake as the sun bows to the sea
To rest, I feel grave for a grave.

Leprosy 1684
Your head was bowed, while hunched, you sat to sob
A baby clenched so tightly in your arms
Lifeless now qualms balms to balm embalm
Denial defile clutch hopes lost dream
Before the eyes
What was has been.

For as the sun sump sinks into the oceans breast, Bina
Takes another child
One mother's timeless quest.

Dressed in black beneath the stars
What would and could have been
Yet what God gives from love's own dream
Is taken to redeem.

On a shooting star
A child is born
Deaths door
Sun-set
Sun-rise
As a mother sobs and cries and cries
'Lord to me why have you lied'

Roderick the Impostor 1697

The girl was standing naked beneath a dammed-up waterfall. She was about 18 years of age with long black hair which flowed over her shoulders and breasts. Her skin was as white as snow and trembled from the shivering of her fear.

All the villagers were assembled to watch the girl's public humiliation. Standing tall and strong, next to the frail young whimpering girl, was the towering figure of 'Roderick the Great', a fiery red haired giant of a man. Roderick was a native of St. Kilda and a self appointed minister to the islanders. His physical size, strength and climbing skills were held in awe, while his determination and forthright nature was not to be contested by any of the passive islanders. His voice was deep dark and foreboding, "*Standing afore ye is a sinner who waits to be cleansed by the blessed waters. A sinner who refused to come to me, Roderick the Great, baptised and instructed by none other than the saint, John the Baptist. I remember the day, six years hence, when I was but 18 years of age. 'Twas a day I returned from fishing as the dawn mist stroked the earth. I could hear a heavenly voice which spoke my name and beckoned for me to approach. 'Have no fear' sayth the voice, 'for you are the chosen one'. Then thunder roared in the heavens and from a bolt of lightening a holy saint came forth to give unto me holy teachings, 'I am John the Baptist and you are chosen from your people to receive the words of the Lord God in the heavens'. The saint baptised my naked body within the fresh waters from the 'Stream of Virtues'. I was taught the ways of the Lord God which I now bring to you. This girl has refused the cleansing of the baptism from the Lord through the purity of mine anointment with the blessed oil to her naked body. I will now bless the waters above her heathen soul that they may flow and wash all evil from her ungrateful body which has been denied my sacred touch. As the waters of heaven are released I will bless them with a Holy psalm".*

The dammed-waters were released over the shivering naked girl, who screamed from the sudden shock of the gushing cold water-fall. "SEE! *How the girl screams as the evil spirits are washed asunder back into hell,*
    Mine is the kingdom of the God Almighty
    Wash and baptise this simple girl

> *That she may be cleansed of evil*
> *Let the Holy Spirit enter her body*
> *And sanctify her lost soul*
> *And bring her spirit back to the kingdom of God.*
> *AMEN".*

AMMMMMMMMMMMMMN

Roderick composed his own psalms and prayers, forbidding the recital of the Lord's prayer or the Ten Commandments. He created new laws and demanded strict fasting on Fridays and a new way of killing sheep without the use of a knife. Through the use of confession he gained the peoples trust and became a powerful figure amongst the islanders. Having the gift of poetry, Roderick held long prayer meetings and sang long rhyming psalms. He christened a piece of land 'John's Hillock' declaring that the land had been consecrated by St John the Baptist and was to be known as 'Holy Ground'. He also declared that a bush upon the hill was sacred and that if any cow or sheep should tread on, or eat from the bush, then the animal was to be slaughtered and eaten by the creature's owner and himself.

The islanders eventually became suspicious of Roderick, and of his intentions and laws, *"From this day the bodies of the departed shall be buried with their heads facing to the South, and not to the East".*

"But! Lord Roderick the Great, it is our ancient burial custom to......."

"Do you dare to question God's will, if the dead are buried with their heads facing south, their spirits will ride away to heaven upon white horses".

Roderick composed a special hymn that was for women only and which he declared would protect them from death during childbirth. If a woman required to be blessed by the hymn, she had to pay Roderick one sheep for the privilege.

The secret ritual had to be performed in private.

"My Holy Lord Roderick I come to you for the blessing as I am with child and pray for a safe birth".

"Bless you my child. Remove your clothes so that I may anoint your body with the sacred oil".

"But! Lord, I feel shame to be naked".

"There is no shame in the eyes of the kingdom of heaven my child, now remove your clothes that I may anoint your body".

"OH! Lord your hands are warm and slippery, OOO NO! Not their Lord!........

"You must obey the Lord, or the wrath of God will place you beneath the cleansing of the blessed waters. Listen to the sacred hymn my child and succumb to God"

So
Deep
The love
To enter into
Your soul's desires
With blessed oils to stroke
The evil from your skin
Mother and Child
My hand will
Bless and
Protect
From
All

WHISPERING WHISPERS WHISPERING WHISPERS

'SSSHT   SSSHT   SSSHT'

I   S   L   A   N   D   E   R   S

Martin Martin	is to visit	soon	YES!	He may help us	be rid of
Roderick	is cursed	a witch	he	will, will the sea	a storm
To be banished	forever	be gone	never	never to return	then peace
Tell tale to Martin	to go	peace	will	not bother us	again
To take Roderick	away	and	be	gone	forever
To Dunvegan	for ever	calm	back	forever	AMEN

AAAAAAAAAAAMMMMMMMMMMEEEEEEEEEEENNNNNNNNNNN

'SSSHT   SSSHT   SSSHT'

Martin Martin's Visit 1697 (1ˢᵗ June)

I fell into a peaceful sleep
To awake......OH! No sounds of waves to greet me
AH! I know this place, the smell of ancient wood and stone.
Dunvegan castle.
Why am I here?
Are my tales from Kilda done?
I hear voices!
I drift to find
Some endless rest from sleep.

Martin Martin	**Chief MacLeod**
The Galley is made ready to sail Sir	Good Man!
I have the Rent tally for Kilda Sir	Good Man! One other problem
What be that Sir?	This.....Roderick
AH! A powerful influence	on the island
A self declared 'Man of God'	from what I hear an impostor
The islanders hold him in awe	AH! And a bully, I have been told
His climbing skills are many	upon the crags
And he possesses the strength of many men,	strong willed
What of the Man Sir?	He has renounced the scriptures
AH! Sacrilege	He has forbidden the Lord's prayer
A sin my Lord	and the recital of the Ten Commandments
Sinner	and I have news of his abuse of women
He's a scoundrel Sir	I'll have nae more of this skulduggery
What be your orders Sir?	He must stand before the presbytery
Aye Sir	and be judged for his crimes
I will bring him before you Sir	And be takin' a hand O sturdy men
Aye Sir, he has the strength of many	And the devil I warrant.

"Captain"
"Yes Mr Martin".
"Be choosin' a crew o' sturdy men, for it'll be the devil this trip we will be a facin'".

Through the morning mist, like a ghostly ship lost
Figure white with towering sails
The Galley crept
To meet
With
God
Or
Devil
Only fate
Command the
Hand of destines cost,
Found renowned astound
Ambivalence, desire, love lust trust lost.

Martin Martin, Steward to MacLeod of Dunvegan castle shouted to his crew as the galley slid up the ageless beach dripping from an ebbing tide. "Make fast and unload the provisions, then be loading the stock for the levy and I'll be havin' nae foul-mouthing or blaspheming, or the whip will taste yer skin".

Martin Martin	**Finlay Gillies**
Be sharing a beer with me	AH! That I will Sir
Here be a list for the rent	Thank ye' sir
43 bolls barley	Yes!
20 stones feathers	Yes!
10 cheese bags	Yes!
10 butter bags	Yes!
Salted sea birds	Yes!
2 barrels gannets	Yes!
4 barrels fulmar	Yes!
1 gallon bird oil	Yes!
You seem dour Finlay	Sir!
Be a worry on yer brow	A cuss it is Sir
What cuss be that, may I ask?	'Tis Roderick Sir
AH! What skulduggery now?	The people have seen his lies
What be?	The sheep from his cousin Muldonich
–	ate from the sacred bush on John's Hillock
–	Roderick told he would be struck down dead
–	yet nought did happen.

Roderick has been summoned
To appear before the Presbytery
If he is found to be an impostor
He will not return to Kilda

OH!
Will we be rid of him?
A sinner
tae sin.

Martin Martin   Roderick the Impostor

How are you Sir? I am with the Lord God Sir, how be yourself?
I am in good health Sir   As am I
Chief MacLeod has asked you visit   AH! He needs confession
His needs are between you and he   AH! I am busy
Yet I feel his mood is dour   with God's work here
His word is a command Sir   I am only commanded by God
God or devil if all be told   Watch your tongue Man
'Tis an order you must obey   What devilment is at hand here
I believe that question will be put to you Sir, Be dammed Man
"GUARDS"

Six strong guards
Wrestled Roderick to the ground
His red hair flayed from a screaming scull,
"Let me go you Heathens or ye will be dammed tae burn in hell"
Islanders ran to cower and hide from Roderick's cuss
Lest be their fate truth call bad luck.

Chained and tied in the galley's keep
Roderick's roars creep waters mists,
As the islanders watched and kneeled to pray
Pure fear in the heart
Should he return one day.

Roderick the Impostor
Roamed the Isle of Skye
Repenting sins sad masquerade
Confess regret
Crimes shadows cowls cast shade.

The Calends Yelling

New Years Eve 2005
I pass the invisible divide
And rest to sleep
Within my cottage roofed room.

I stare through the skylight window
The stars of 2006 remain the same
Nothing seems to have changed
Except time.

Wine and Whiskey
May spin minds gates free
For just one night of escape.

Deep sleep sink to rest in peace
NO! Not I
I try to stay awake
Fear, yes Fear
For dreams dream away the endless night
Carried by some?
Time trap trapped wrap wrapped warp warped *Taish* seer seeing.

Shall I wake, to rebel? Refuse to write? Tell Tales to tell no more?
Face feelings of guilt, some compulsion, the unknown to know
Ignorance is bliss? What you do not know cannot harm you?
To die on your feet, or to live on your knees?
For I feel soon Dark Waves Storm approaching
READER! Take your chance and go
For soon tthheee
eeee
eeeeeeeeeee......................

Hersht......Heersht......Hersht

I awake to find myself standing by the whispering sea.
The armies ranks of waves reflecting the moonlight
Silver streaks strewn endless lines
Of whispers past now waiting
Existing, forever?
To be read
Through
Tales
To
Tell

A group of people were huddled together with some cows. There was a very excited atmosphere. The people were giggling and whispering to each other. I approached the group to find that the people were young; between fourteen and twenty years of age. The boys and girls were busy tying strips of raw-hide onto the end of long sticks, while one lad was being covered by a full cow's skin. One of the older boys shouted instructions to the lad dressed in the cow hide, *"Now! Remember you must run around each house the way of the sun three times, for each house must have good luck for the New Year".*

Suddenly there was a mighty uproar of noise from the youngsters, as they proceeded to chase the lad covered in the raw hide. The lad ran mooing, like a cow in stress, as the remaining youths chased him whilst whipping his hide with the tassels tied to the end of their sticks. *"MOOOOOO...MOOOOOO"*, cried the boy as about twelve boys and girls whipped his hide, for leather, whilst shouting and chanting, *"Let us raise the noise louder, let us beat the hide".*

After running around each house, 'the way of the sun' three times, the frantic group stood waiting at the door of the home. When the door was opened the crowd pushed in and sang there chant, *"May God bless this house and all that belong to it, cattle, stones and timber. May it abound with meat and food and clothes and a fertile bed and may good health be in this house."*

Each of the youths then dipped the tassels from the end

of their sticks into the flames of the peat fire and a smouldering piece of hide was then touched to each person and animal's nose living in the household, as another ritual chant is made, *"Good Luck for the New Year."*

After the New Year ceremony was completed cakes were handed to the visitors, who quickly ran off to start their ritual of good luck at the next house.

The Bannock Cake Barley Wine Dance

Happy New Year, 'tis New Years Day
And in the hall the table is laid
Where rests a crown of rock
As bold as a boulder stone block
And the stacs seem to blink and then wave.

The biggest barley cake, as ever was seen
Under its weight the table's legs scream
Sunlit light
Golden bright butter churn
Be as broad as the stone of the quern.

Cheese and wine and an old twisting line
And a fiddler's long bow's haunting whine
Be a brown wooden flute
And a black dancing boot
Dance steps for the young 'un's to learn
Spin left and then right now cheer with delight
Be as broad as the stone of the quern.

New Years Days
Pure romance
Everyone sings and chants
'Tis the
Bannock Cake Barley Wine Dance.

The Cavalcade

Silhouettes across the western sunrise
Black horses heads manes wafting breeze
Stomping hooves anticipating, tease
Riders suddenly shouting wave
'Tis the charging cavalcade.

Low riders sandy dust cloud high
From the beach to Village Bay
Wild horses ride the raging wind
With beating hooves grinds grounds thunder sway.

Fifty men on a bare back ride
The devil for to play
Screaming skulls in a race, parade
'Tis the charging cavalcade.

The horses noose
One length of rope wrapped around a fist
While one arm wrestles with the breeze
As the stacs sigh, ill at ease.

Some men fall while some ride tall
Be the hooves beat pounding thunder
Only one may win the race
To take the champions plunder.

In a wave from a beach
Kick the dust sands salt
Ride the tide
Ebb the eve times flow
Froth white in the night
White horses plight
Spit the grit
Bite the bridles bow.

'Tis the crags man's ride through the gates of hell
Being only for the brave
One man back on a horse's back
'Tis the charging cavalcade.

The Cragsmen

I awake to deep dark fear
Swirling black mists kissed death's last wish
For a hell to know
This fear surrounds
As pounding heart
Needs be escape to meet and end?

I hold my head,
Covering ears and eyes
As if to stop some impending... what?
For we all must sleep
And walk some way
To where? Who says?
The hope, to wake, next day.

I was standing high upon *stac Armin*. I felt confused. I had just fallen into a deep sleep, to awake into some kind of nightmare. I had passed through swirling black foreboding mists to find myself standing on one of the old man's tiers. It was a beautiful day, the sun was shining and the sea was sparkling to hide depths of the oceans greens to blue, as if some artist's paint pots mixed, tipped, entwined a ghostly dance to hue.

Father and two sons were climbing stac *Armin*. They wreathed like snakes, curling and creeping up the mountain's sheer cold face. They moved like stalking wild cats, feeling with naked toes and finger-tips for cracks, crannies or shapes of lips to ledges ridges grips. The three were linked together with a rope and the Father of the two sons led the way. There were bags hanging from there waists that swung like pendulums. Their skill was a sight to behold as they climbed higher and higher, travelling up the face of stac *Armin*.

Sweat dripped from creased brows furrows as the three moved as one, a team spent a life time's skills to exalt souls passion, dangers universal dream.

Something was instantly wrong. A startled bird had flown from the cliff and smashed into the trailing son's face. He missed his grip and started to fall. The young man shouted loudly to alert his brother and father who were above him. The boy fell through the air several yards before the rope made a loud whipping sound as it took the sudden strain of his now dangling body. The fallen son swung slowly from left, then to right, holding onto his lifeline. The father of the boys shouted to his son who remained on the rock's face, "*Swing him in! Swing him in!*"

The boy gripped a ledge with one hand as he reached down to swing the rope which held his dangling brother. The rope started to swing as the boy at the end of the line swung like a pendulum, kicking through the air with his legs to gain more momentum. The dangling youth grasped for a ledge and shouted loudly, "*YES!*" as he felt his fingers slide into a crevice of life.

Suddenly success turned into a nightmare. The son who was swinging his brother below while holding a ledge with one hand screamed with fear. The ledge he had been holding onto came away. He instantly fell toward his brother who had just regained his grip. Too late, the two sons fell from the cliff face and were left dangling in oblivion.

The boys' father was left gripping with all his strength, clawing at the stac's surface like a flea on the skin of a scratching beast.

Within a moment the son next in line to his father took a knife from his belt and started to cut the rope in front of his face. His father screamed, "***NO NO NO***". The rope snapped and as the two boys fell to meet with death on the hungry rocks below, the son's voice echoed a cry around the pinnacles haunting stacs, "*Father, I love you*".

I watched helplessly as the grief stricken father clung weeping on the cliff's face and I am sure he was deciding if he too should let go of life and join his lost sons.

Eventually the father completed the climb to the top of stac *Armin,* where he lay upon his back for many hours sobbing and thumping the cold hard rock. He looked down at the busy sea, possibly denial, some hope that his sons may still be alive; swimming and laughing. All that was to be seen was the twirling gannets, oblivious of the pain of loss.

The father sat for a long time with his head sunk into his hands. Eventually he rose to his feet and started to climb down stac *Armin*. His dissent was care free, as if to fall may be a relief from his pain of loss.

As he eventually reached the bottom of Armin, the father of the boys found a length of rope, and a gannet with the remains of a short length of rope tied to its legs. He looked for his sons, but the tide had stolen all hope. The heartbroken father stood as if frozen, holding the gannet and the rope whilst staring out to sea.

As day turned into night he remained, possibly waiting for the next tide, when, may be, his two sons would be returned by the hand of Neptune's grace.

I left the man with sorrow for my heart did ache.

Armin was indifferent and none compliant.
For today is today
And tomorrow will be the same as yesterday
For only people come and then go.

TALES FROM THE CARDING PARTIES

Heersht......Heersht......Heersht
I awoke slowly.
I covered my eyes with my hands.
My last visit to Kilda had been a nightmare.
I had several sleepless nights
Ghostly taps creaking floorboards shadows cast
I felt death had been all around me
I prayed I would never again have to return
and witness such sorrow
Heersht......Heersht......Heersht
The waves whisper, RELAXxxxxxxxxxxx
I slowly open my eyes and turn my head
I see the old man's crowned pinnacles
The same, as ever was, today, to be.

I walked amongst the bleak black houses, for the whispers led me astray. White bird feathers were covering the damp soiled ground between the houses. 'Twas like snow which floated, twirled then played within the wisps of the breeze. Suddenly a barking dog flew towards me to pass through my floating spirit, it instantly spun around yelped and cowered away bewildered.

Between the cracks of the stone-built walls a variety of dead birds were hanging by their beaks. These unfortunate birds had been crammed into the gaps of the masonry.

The smell made me feel sick. I looked at the brightly coloured beak of a puffin which was stuck into the wall. The bird hung, as if trapped, as if it had flown into the wall by mistake and become stuck, then died slowly.

I shook my head to wake, a waste of time. The stench was terrible. The smell was of a mixture of sewage, rotting food and animal waste.

I walked toward a door where the whispers were coming from. I entered the room to find it full of people, mostly women.

The people were sitting on stools, stones and wooden chests and they drank some sort of 'Barley wine' as they chatted and laughed freely. The room was small and all the islanders were squashed together.

There must have been about thirty people in the tiny room. I was aware of the communal spirit between the group. It was as if they were all one family, everything was shared and everyone was looked after by all.

I noticed the floor was covered in trodden waste which consisted of food skins, dung, ashes from the peat-fire, and a variety of other different substances. Wooden boards rested against the walls which were covered in wool and had long pronged wooden combs stuck into them ready for further use.

A young boy shouted out *"Tales! Tales! Tell Tales!"* The people in the room became silent as an elderly lady began to speak. Her face was dark and deep from the lines of time, where wisdom flows to creep, *"AHHHHAAA, laddy"*. The boy cringed from fear as the old woman grasped his arm with claw-like talons, and began to talk in a cackling high pitched screech, *"I'll be telling ye a tale laddie, AHHHHAA, be the tale of the 'Gift o' the Gab' AHHHHAAA, is that what ye have lad? AHHHHAA, The Gift O' the Gab? AHHHAAAAAAAAAA..............*

The Gift O' the Gab
One day when the sun was shining bright
Two beautiful fairy women
Danced within a floating dream
Their long fair hair to tease a breeze
Silken gowns of flowing green.

Collecting 'mothan', magic herb
Each leaf kissed stroking palm
Placed within their baskets deep
To take home, mix a magic charm.

Weary from a playful day
Their baskets laid to rest
They skip and dance
Sing of romance
Be the fairies true loves quest.

Wishing a dream from a
Wishing well
Some handsome prince to woo
Drink deep fair maids for all may be
From the old 'Well of Virtue'.

While the maids drank deep
From the wishing well
A nanny-goat passed by
Sweet smell the 'mothan'
Magic leaves
Twinkle bright in the goat's left eye.

Munching, crunching, chewing the cud
The once thin goat
Found the herb feast good
She wobbled left and she wobbled right
Yet she was so fat
That her legs stuck tight.

The fairies caught the nanny-goat
And tied a rope around her shoulder
Where she chewed the cud as her head did buzz
Tightly tied to a heavy boulder.

For her milk was magic
From the herb 'mothan'
Not for mortal folk to drink
So the fairies milked her every day
Then poured it down a sink.

One day a mighty storm passed by
And the goat's rope tugged and rubbed and snapped
And the goat escaped through an old bent gate
Running free, be the goat's own spate.

The storm passed by as the sun peeped low
And the goat hid by a wall
As the fairies lurked with a silver birch
They cried and wailed and searched.

Outside the walls of a bleak black house
The bleating nanny-goat cried
And a mother with a hungry child
Took the bleating goat inside
"AH! My son will have fresh milk today"
Once gone the devil may pay.

Morag filled her jug with milk
As the goat did huff and puff
And she wondered if the milk was real
Or maybe a nanny-goat's bluff.

Morag's son was but three years of age
And he drank the milk with glee
And his eyes spun around
As he laughed and cried
He had never been so happy.

The fairies saw the nanny-goat
Standing by a black house with a grin
With an open door
They looked for more
And they found the boy within.

Morag shouted "Who are you?"
And with a wave of a magic hand
The mother's voice was lost forever
She was frozen and could not stand.

The fairies gave the boy a gift
From the magic which he held inside
'The Gift O' the Gab'
For a chosen lad
Forever speaking
Magic words
And poems
Laments
Love
Cast
X

The Changeling
West of Village Bay
By Glean Mór hills
The people were working upon the 'Plain of Spells'
Liani nin Ore
Where the cattle were stained with
Salt, Fire and Water.

Mrs Ferguson's son was five years old
And he ran and played as his mother worked
Upon the Plain of Spells
Liani nin Ore
By steep Glean Mór.

Time blessed passed by
For home tae roam
The people returned to Village Bay
And Mrs Ferguson watched her son
As he acted in a peculiar way.

The boy did brood
And he ate no food
And his hair turned white then grey
As he moped and sulked by Glean Mór's brooks
day by day by day
He became very old and thin and yellow
And all in all, all thought him an unusual wee fellow.

The village had a wise old man
With 'second sight' Taish
When he saw the boy
He could sense foul play
From the fairies
Daoine Sith

"It is not your son, I fear
For he has be stolen by the
Daoine Sith
And changed for a
Sibhreach
SEE! Yellow skin and teeth".

Mrs Ferguson cried, and cried, and cried,
"How will I see my son again, I hold me self tae blame
For if I had kept an eye on him
There would have been nae shame".

"Now have nae fear"
The wise man said
"Ye must test tae see if a change be made.
Take two empty old egg-shells
And while the boy is at rest on his bed
Fill the big old cooking pot wi' water
And watch the young laddy's head".

Mother carried two old egg-shells
And to the well she walked and walked
For many hours, and hours and hours
Back and to, fro and fro,
To fill the pot
To overflow.

Suddenly the boy began to laugh, and laugh and laugh
"HAAAAAAAAAAAA HAAAAAAAAAAAAARRRRRR
I am 800 years of age
and I have never seen such a fool as you
HAAAAAAAAAAAA HAAAAAAAAAAAAARRRRRR"

The old wise man was quick to act
"AH! Now light a fire with the wood from the byre
And throw the wee laddie in
For if it be your son he will cry and run
But if the changeling
He will cuss
And disappear in a
Smoky puff".

The fire was bright and the wood was hot
When the laddie was tossed to the middle
And he screamed and cussed
And made a fuss
Then suddenly vanished in a smoky puff.

'Twas the darkest night that ever was
When the wise old man took the mothers hand
And they crept across to the
Plain of Spells
Far across the barren land.

With a dirk and a bible, and a crowing cock
They climbed a grassy hill
Where fairies danced and sang and played
As they marched to a pipes parade.

With the cock standing on his shoulder
The old wise man stood tall and proud
As the crow crowed long and hard and loud
With the bible held in his raised right hand
While his left hand's fist
Carried the dirk in it
Be the devil
For tae kiss.

"Gee me the boy ye have stolen
Return him tae me now,
Or the bibles dirk
Be the cockerel curse
Tae cast upon yer brow".

The fairies trembled, frozen with fear
For such a sight they had never seen
And the stolen boy heard his mother's cry
And he began to
Scream and Scream.

And suddenly the boy ran free
And they all ran home together
And they laughed and danced forevermore
Upon the purple heather.

The Water Bull

Three young lad's on Boreray
Were collecting birds as was their way
They drifted down to find a lonely beach
Where beneath a giant rock of old
Was a deep black cave
And the air was freezing cold.

"AH!" said one "Am nae goin' in there"
Said another "BAH! Be the devil tae scare"
And his brother shouted "I'll go anywhere"

The air was cold like frozen ice
While far above the sun shone
Hot and bright,
And albeit a bright and sunny day
Within the cave was a foreboding darkness
Be the bravest for to sway.

The boys crept forward
One by one
As each one watched the other one
For if one be taken, which one be?
The other one? AH! Then one goes free.

Standing within 'twas dark and freezing
Deep feelings, evil mists
From the devil's own foul breathing
The pungent repugnant hiss
Be the smell of death
For lust's last kiss
Drops drool dripping wet
Across the face between the lips
Time past, turn back, regret.

Steep steps stepping
Creep creep creepy creeping
Testing the devil's own
Only once to be one meeting.

AHHHHHHHHHHHHHHHHHHAAAAAAAAAAAAAAAA

Suddenly a pair of deep red sunken eyes

And a roar as deep as thunder
Pounding galloping chasing hooves
The boys did run asunder.

One ran left and one ran right
One ran into the sea
And he swam so hard, and he swam so fast
He swam around 'stac lee'
And never such a sight was seen
As the three bold boys did flee.

As the moon did fly high over Skye
The three boys returned into their bothy
And all swore to return home
Come dawn next day
Home safe to Village Bay.

The three boys drank sweet barley wine
And the bothy walls did spin
And they spoke of dreams
Things never seen
And they spoke of a dream
which each had seen
foretold to now redeem.

'Spoke one'
"I like a woman with long Black Hair!"
Suddenly a knock was on the bothy door
And the lad did creep to see
A beautiful woman with long black hair
Flowing free just like the sea
And her skin was white
In the pale moonlight
This was his dream to be.

'Spoke two'
"I like a woman with long Red Hair!"
Suddenly a knock was on the bothy door
And the lad did creep to see
A beautiful woman with long red hair
Flowing free just like the sea
And her skin was white
In the pale moonlight
This was his dream to be.

'Spoke three'
"I like a woman with long Blonde Hair!"
Suddenly a knock was on the bothy door
And the lad did creep to see
A beautiful woman with long blonde hair
Flowing free just like the sea
And her skin was white
In the pale moonlight
This was his dream to be.

And lust did creep
As the boys did peep
And each looked to each the other
For the one to test
Dream's eternal quest
For to find a
Perfect lover.

The three drew feathers
For to see
Who the bravest boy would be
And the shortest quill
Would soon find out
What lust loves dreams fulfil.

Three feathers drawn
For the devil's spawn
For what to be will be
Too young to love
Lust's taste of fruit
Succumb, desires destiny.

One boy peeps through
The door-jam's crack
And stares into his truelove's eyes
He stretches out his trembling hand
To stroke her pure white thighs.

She beckons to him with
Pursed red lips
Sweet soft subtle suckle shuffle
Shy? How? Why?
Pure innocence incensed impetuous imp
The Black Widow's
Death watch sigh.

The creaking croaking aching door
As if a cry scream screeching doubt
The mind to think
Pure lust...no doubt
The soul turned inside out.

Outside the bothy
Two boys now peep
For what will be
Hopes dreams nae weep.

Into the woman's outstretched arms
The boy did walk to hold and kiss
For dreams come true forever more
Be the devil's own last wish.

And as their lips, so softly met
Under the moonlight's beams that glow
The boy felt heaven in his grasp
Be the hell he did not know.

Her tongue slid down his open throat
And her eyes turned fiery red
For the devil's lust, lusts endlessly
For lost souls filled with dread.

As the two boys watched and stared
The woman turned into
A mighty water bull
And tossed their friend upon its horns
To sever rip and pull.

The boys closed tight the bothy door
And the beast did charge and bang and roar
With ice for breath and fiery eyes
Be the devil's beastly cries.

All night long the bull did roar
Charging, battering at the door
Until the bothy walls
Could take no more
Be the devil's own to score.

SUDDENLY
At last!
The sun began to rise
And an old cock crowed
The golden dawn
And the water bull
Returned to its grave
Be the old wet dark cold cave
Where the darkest sins of all begin
'Tis the sinners sin din d jinn.

Just after dawn at Village Bay
The people stood to stare in awe
For one big wave
Was on its way
One wave, alone at the break of day.

Suddenly behind the wave
A little boat was seen
Be two lads rowing
For life or death
From nightmares
One true
Dream.

The Well of Youth
Tobar na h-oige. The Well of Youth.

An old man took a lonely walk
For time ticks by
And never waits
Be the time of birth, or a time to die
No answer as to why
And yet the long days, day's eve
The old man knew his time was nigh
When some answer?
As to why time fly
With the sun to moon each day pass by
Be death's own whispers sigh.

And as he walked the lonely path
Where we all will walk one time
His foot did slip upon the grass
While above the sun did shine
And as he fell
His lost soul laughed
For a lifetime seen, be one second of his past.

Then suddenly he could see a well
A wishing well? Possibly?
So he walked to see what he may see
For a wish sometimes be free.

And around the well were beautiful flowers
Of pink and blue, golden yellow, and red with a violet hue
And sweet perfume was all around
As butterflies danced rainbows dreams
Between peaceful glowing sunlit beams.

The old man looked into the well
Where a milky-white liquid flowed like cream
And his thirst was such that he had to taste
Of the white sweet cream and honey
For his lips did kiss
This heavenly bliss
Be his soul sink listless moony.

After a time, as time fly by
The old man danced and felt so free
From aching bones
And weary legs
And his eyes now clear could see.

He felt as a child, and danced and danced
And ran and jumped
And swam and rolled down hills
And climbed the taunting high stac lee
For he had never felt so free.

He ran to tell of the
Well of Youth
To all at Village Bay
To take them so they might drink of life
And dance the day away.

Once at the Village
The old man
Danced and ran and jumped for joy
And the people set to walk the hills
And with the children skipping
The old man did play
Fairy rings spinning wishes sway.

Eventually they found the spot
Where the Well of Youth once was
Now on the spot
Where the well once stood
Lay the old man at peace with God.

And the people knelt and prayed and cried
Yet no one could understand
How time lost past
Be an hour glass
To simply turn
As the last grain pass.

The Stone of Knowledge
Clach an Eolas.
Old alter lain slain through endless hopes
Where wishers dreams link magic sacrificial gifts
As pointing stacs wait reaching for the sky
Some drowning claw forever froze
But one last grasp clasp gasp.

Deity sobriety
Or chaos bedlam anarchy
Pandemonium tumult Pandora
For dancing Gods infinity, finite?
For even Gods will
Wills the night
To wonder
Was I right?

Who dares to see?
Who needs to know?
For the morrow come
As the last day go.

The first day of the moon's new romance
Clach an Eolas
Standing upon the rock of ages
Stealing secret signs from key holes peeping
Narcissism narcosis neurosis
Seeing tomorrow's, all, for now
Second sight
A blip in time
To

J
U
M
P

One Line...

TAISH

The Milking Stone
The Milking Stone. Clach a' Bhainne

Beneath the mighty Milking Stone
Amidst the first spring milking
The fairies danced with tinkling spoons
Waiting for a gift for drinking.

By the moonlight bright
Through the depths of night
Pour the milk upon the Milking Stone
SSSHHH!
You will hear the fairies as they slurp
Pure elixirs white tonic.

The fairies dance upon the stone
To skip the light fandango
To laugh with glee
As they twirl so free
'Tis the fairies white milk spree.

Watch out for the Gruagach
Seen standing on the stone
His long hair blowing in the wind
As he laughs with a haunting groan.

For if he sips his milk on Sundays
It will quell his cuss on Mondays
For if he has his Sunday treat
Good luck will reign all week.

The milking stone
Where the milk flows free
For the fairies for to drink
To bring good luck
Flowing every day
From the Gruagach
Grumpy grampus gourmet.

On Sea and On Land

The galleys raced with sails adrift tied free
To blow the gales tae rift
The belching, wailing, slapping canvas craft tied fly,
Across a heaving sea.

The two ships side by side to ride the bucking waves
As several sailors fell tae sea
Tae kiss the swift mermaid.

The ships smashed into fist full wistful waves
A list full sea green deep blue grave
To climb then drop to slop and flop
To fight through the beating rain.

Captain MacDonald and Captain MacLeod
Rode the waves in their two ships
Standing as figure-heads so proud,
Be a race to St. Kilda
With honour on a line
Sea wrecked lives, one winner for all time.

The land be near, be the rocks nae fear
Crashing bashing splintering wood
The captains' rage the heaving waves
"Sail on, sail on, 'til ye all be in yer graves"

The two ships sailing side by side
Almost on land, the first man touch the land the winner,
The weather turn to calm sea glass
Nae breeze tae blow, the last wave splash.

Instantly still the two forlorn and battered ships
To oars to row to 'get to grips'
When suddenly Captain MacLeod chops his left hand free,
To throw to land
While laughing aloud
"The first on land the winner be, beat by a hand MacDonald,
Let my motto now forever stand
'On sea and on the land'

(From poetic tales from the Isle of Skye)

The Burning of the Church

Hundreds of year's time past
When most of the islanders were visiting Long Island
Two rogues from Lewis
Duigan and Fearchar mòr
Became shipwrecked on St. Kilda.

Mischievous wayward rogues
With fire flints steel, steal thieves thrive
Tempestuous temptress trespass
For nought to take to keep to reap......some trophy?
Nothing to avoid but space
Within voids endless timeless keep
For the stacs tower high and nae look down nor back
And through the silence, solitude
Emancipation's mirror, cruel and cracked narcissistic glass
Through degeneration endowed emancipation?
Urobors
Circular serpent's head to tail devouring the fool
Swallowing ones self to create one self
For I, to be I, everything,
Then what?
OH!
Nothing

Two bad men climb Aois-mheall
To look for what?
Some secret ghosts the chill may hide
For the old man's wisdom
Often sighs
Be not for restless eyes.

Some Love to Hate
Some need to Hate
Some Hate to Hate
So Hate, Hate for Hating Hate.

Duigan and Fearchar mòr return from climbing Aois-mheall
To shout a lie
"Quickly people hide in the church
the ships of the Sassenachs approach"

Once all were safe? Inside.
The evil men fastened the door
Then burnt the little chapel down
Until there was no sound.

One woman who was far away
Could see the rising twisting smoke
And crept back by a secret way
For to spy on Village Bay.

She could see the two men dance with glee
By the smoke from a devil's hell
And she realised all her friends were dead
Yet she had no one to tell

And she did not know nor understand
Such evil hateful ways
So she took to hide out in the hills
For days, and days, and days.

After time passed by
The Stewart, from MacLeod was seen to be approaching
The island.

Duigan and Fearchar mòr
"OH! Kind sir, there has been a terrible happening, for we were shipwrecked and swam to the island, only to find everyone burnt within the church"

Suddenly the woman who had been hiding, ran to the Stewart and his men, who had returned with islanders from
St. Kilda.

"Lord, Lord, Please help me, thank God you have returned
for these two evil men have burnt the church
with all the people trapped inside"
The two evil men were seized and held to count
For there evil deeds
And their punishment was for to be
Abandoned high on Stac-an-àrmin
With nought to eat but raw bird meat.

And Fearchar mòr could not bear his exiled existence
For lonely evil souls flames from hell caress, for to burn in
A meticulous patient licking way
Upon the old mans stacs which never move nor sway.

Fearchar's mind spun wild
From webs to weave
From hunger's greed
And soon he could bear no more
So took a chance to take a leap
To sea to see
If a boat be in the keep.

Fearchar mòr
Was seen nae more
For the wheel of life
Has a timeless score
To sow to reap the past repeat
To turn as the earth from dark to light
And as the earth revolves around the sun
The seasons come then go
From the budding of the seeds of life
To the crisp trodden leaves in snow.

And Duigan
Sunk into some mindless depths
Escape?
Regret forget
And he built a wall to ease the North Wind
Onto which he carved his name
Which until this day
Does still remain.

Duigan

The Cave of the Irishman

One Christmas morning lifetimes past
Was an Irishman with a wooden cask
And in a boat the two did float
Be the rye row till 'tis dry.

And he saw an isle with pointed stacs
And he drifted wide and he drifted back
Until he reached a sandy shore
And his thirst could take nae more.
Be the rye row till 'tis dry.

And he saw some cliffs
With a cave below
So he crept inside tae hide
Be where no one know
And he opened up his wooden cask
And he dinnae fear as he had nae glass.
Be the rye row till 'tis dry.

And he drank all day
And he drank all night
And he danced on the sand
While the moon shone bright
And the stars did spin
With pure delight
Be the dance
Of the dance
Of Life.

And he drank by day, and he drank by night
For twelve months from the cask
And time flew by sae fast
For every day was as the last
And he never wondered how or why
Be the rye row till 'tis dry.

One year Christmas past
And the Irishman sailed home
With an empty cask
Be the rye now drunken dry.

The Seal Woman

From the land beneath
The deep green sea
The other world
'Tir fó Motifs' land under waves
Seals swim and splash
In underwater caves.

One sunny day young Donald MacDonald
Was collecting eggs from Soay
And he lay to rest, to feel the warm sun upon his face and chest.
He watched the birds like twirling snowflakes
Spinning spirals rising up to adorn the wrinkled stacs.

Donald watched as a Great Auk, clumsily walked along a ledge
Then dived into the sea to swim like a fish beneath the waves,
And as he watched the splendour of the bird,
a seal appeared and swam as if to play,
and the two chased fish
like lightening
flashes
startling cuts
gashes silver blades
florescence bright licked
luminous turquoise torques
wrestling games in endless waves
to jump through the air then splash dive
plummet sump gulp chasms caesium caesurae
Instantly frozen still as in a solid sea, nectars rhapsody
Suddenly swimming again so free.

As young Donald MacDonald
Lazily lay watching the seal and bird at play
The two jumped from the waves
And the seal upon the rocks close by
Did lie upon its back
And as Donald watched
He could not believe his eyes
As its skin began to crack.

As a cocoon, some butterfly free soaking solar waves
Emerging arms, pull twisting, gasping airs first breath of life
As black hair flows rising to meet the warm sifting breeze
Like smokes incense incensed perfume
Drifts to the young man's nose
To breathe so deep his soul to weep
For such a nectar be a gift
To a lowly soul bereft.

Pulling free tumultuous amphibious
Birth's first pain
Crystal's chrysalis transforming dreams
White skin turns red to brown
Outstretched upon a sea-weed strewn boulder smooth
The naked water nymph
Greets floating clouds
With trembling lips
Searching the unknown
Be loves first sweetest kiss.

The young man stares with open mouth
And unblinking eyes
Perchance to miss one second
From listless paradise.

Such beauty he had never before known
So free?
So wild?
A woman yet? A child?

Long stretching legs
Leading to hips curved flowing under velvet soft brown skin
To waiting waist lines sculptured, God's own effigy?
Nature's mountains, milky streams of dripping life
From cheery buds sweet suckling nipples gifted gift rift lips kiss
Warm woman's love to hold, caress, heaven?
How close, Eurynome, Dione, Hebe,
Upon a rock of Hirta
Rests the pearl of destiny.

Her eyes deep sunken green to swallow
Quickly! Steal one fleeting glance
AH! Forever lost spin in drunken ecstasy, let go of all
To catch romance and bring a man to an angel's harmony
For wishes wished dreams kissed blest bliss
One thousand million times, impregnation manifest, from hope
From black rocks cracks spit jewels gold diamond gems
The oyster's virgin lips open wide agape create, one pearl
Aphrodite, golden goddess of love decrees
Daughter of Ouranos
Foam, foam of the foaming seas.

MacDonald stares for many hours, a statue worshiping beauty
As if one eye to blink may wake from sleep's, slept past dream.
One movement may wake the butterfly, fly by
Then who believe, a young boy's dreams
For fantasy and destiny the line of fate create
Can one moment last forever?
Within the presence of the gods
If in his image
Should we wait?
Perchance one chance escape
Torturous Eros If? If? If?
???????????????
Courage, anticipate the last debate.

Donald moves from his hiding place
With gentle steps and smiling eyes
Walking towards the beauty from the sea.
Beneath the satin skies
She, startled, jumps
Panic or curiosity?
Life or Death?
Love or mundane existence?
She watches frowning frowns brows brow
For something
Wonder, wondrous wandering
Perchance a prince
This handsome youth
Some answer to
Prevail the wreaths of truth.

The Seal Woman *and the* **Youth**

Who are you?	*Who are you?*
I am from the caves beneath the sea	*I am from the stacs*
Where the ocean meets the crown	*of kings*
The pinnacles first lament	*hell bound bent.*
Your smile is kind	*Your eyes have endless depths*
You whisper. Why?	*I fear you will leave me*
I am here now	*my eyes have tears*
So do not cry	*your beauty*
Nor wonder how	*I have wished and dreamed*
'Tis fate we meet	*for one moment or an eternity*
So take this time	*to meet with your tranquillity*
Please hold my hand	*Your skin! So soft and smooth*
Your hands! Rough as crags	*you squeeze my hand*
I feel your strength	*and feel my pain*
You feel alone	*I am looking for love*
And I feel your love	*for only love can live*
Love I have never known	*two lost souls?*
The two as one	*the same.*
Your tears are hot	*you take my pain*
Rest your head	*onto your breasts*
Your tears flow free	*for freedom's love*
Onto my body	*a heart's request*
To drip into the sea	*my salty tears*
Will over-flow one day	*all peoples pain*
Will sink the earth	*to flood without refrain.*
You hold me tight	*please suckle me*
You suck my breast	*to drink from hope*
I feel so weak	*I am your strength*
Between my thighs	*the seed of life*

Can hold no lies.

Hold me tightly
Your love and warmth
Love on a stone cold rock
Yet tears and blood run
Into the sea
From our virginity
Through sacrifice
And take the love
I give
You give

forever
will always be
within the stacs
endlessly
our baptised rock
true love?
I give to you
you take
I give
to take

A circle of life.

And now my love I must go
Down to the caves
Where love and hopes and dreams
Are safe for now from war and pain
So deep the ocean depths to drown
Your spirit will remain with truth rather

please! No!
stay with me
remain
take me
far better to die
than live a lie

Into the seal skin she slipped away into the oceans fathoms deep
For life and love live endlessly
Dreams memories forever keep
From tears and love and pain and joy
The world revolve
Some test? Or game?
For each new day becomes today's yesterday
And each day blames the last, or the next
And as our blood runs into the sea
Somewhere deep down
One love safe lives on endlessly
For when the world is torn asunder
One child remain
To fill a crown
To fill a crown
With
Wonder.

The Empty Carding Room

Heersht......Heersht......Heersht

I wake once more upon the whispering beach
So many nights told tales
'Til dawn day's break
Be quick the quill
To write in haste.

Routine, my stride to the Carding room
And yet this night no whispers be
For in the silence something,
Possibly nothing, waits for me.

Is this the end of Kildar's tales?
Will I be free?
To sleep in peace through floating clouds
To wake caressed within dawn's soft harmony.

The carding room door is open
And three women are standing sadly and silently outside
Within the room is empty and silent.
I feel alone.
All I can remember is the crowded busy room
Where laughter, joy and happiness reigned.

A stir begins as cold as ice
As mists ghosts whisks taunt
Laughter cruel to fool a fool.
I shake my head to wake and wake and wake and........?
Then to wait with fear to sleep...
AH! Go if you wish!
For readers read between the lines
Or skip a miss mistttttttttt.................
zzzzz zzzzzz zzzzz

The Reverend Alexander Buchan 1705

The first to come with all to tell, who knows?
Missionary Man to root the roots new route to-boot
The freedom of a simple soul
To penetrate and loot.

No more Pagan Superstitious Customs
Propagate manipulate and educate
For what you are will be no more
For the laws and rules of mainland land's and Lords
Sure, must be right
God's own eternal score
To justify each
War.

The first manse built
Women and children taught beliefs
The enlightenment of the poor
The need to need needs need no more.

Learn how to knit and sow and weave
To be part of the world you need
For all in all, all will, will will
Alls greed
For all fulfil.

Know right from wrong
And fight the fight
For who interprets
Interpellated right.

1730 Reverend Buchan died
The fever stole away his life
And who knows if the change changed changes
Changed pure innocence and simplicities last chance
Or left the complicated scars of
Demonetized dominions dominance.

Will-O'—The – Wisp

Once more I wake into creeping white mists
Which seem to dance
Silky veils captured within spotlights
Moonlit beams.

Fear is predominant
I feel like hiding, I want to return home,
I shake my head to wake
Suddenly a shape appears so I instinctively run for cover.

Crouching o'er a gravestone cold
In a deep dark moonlit night
With creeping shadows veils to dance
To the devil's sweet delight.

I press against the cold wet stone
Be a chiselled deep-cut line
Be some lost drifting forlorn soul
Buried now, at the edge of time

The thespians final role
As the curtain falls, flails fails to call
All the ghosts have left the hall.

Murky mists kiss starlit beams
And a cuckoo koo's cue the veil's last show
For the dance of death
In the ground below
Where the peat-bog-crag
Seeds grow.

Gill-Chriosd stands cold staring eyes
Oval stone framed guardian
Sepulchre of Jesus Christ
I wonder what your eyes beheld
Within deaths depths
Choirs chime hells bells.

Dirges sung the last lament composed
Weep, howl, wail, curtail the final truths call calling
Winds spirits wisp whispering kissed
Worked wrought preformed performed
The dead deed creed needs
Death's wish hissed
Through hell
To heavens
Gates of
Bliss.

The Banshee howls crying carrions death
Across the grave gravestones
For some poor soul the last gasps breath
Wormed soils bleached ghost white bones.

Will—O'—the—Wisp
Floating light?
From the dying
Moribund in extremis
From home to grave
The death march
Dasyures.

When the west wind blows
The 'Sluagh' Spirit Host' hordes crescent fly
Strayed wayward ghosts phantoms prey
Talons tearing careless, care less to choose souls fools
Gill-Chriosd gaze dazed crazed myriad.

Earth-bound spirits rhapsody
Howling quartet pyrite pirouette pierrot
For eternity
One final curtain call
For the first new born
Be the last to fall.

Smallpox 1727

*Bacillus death's calling
From a dead man's clothes who visited Harris
A gift bag bagged with the devil's own vultures talons
The gift of death, or curse to maul mêlée
Perfection, safe? Vulnerability, waiting
One weak link for the edge of time
Pollution mar pure harmony.*

*Within the stacs stacked graves
Invading death watch days of grief
Malaise, fever, head-aches
A fear beyond belief.*

*Vomit free, spit the demon from within
Who comes to digest lives life line
To eat away at the old man's crust
The reaper reaps
Hiss the sigh of lust.*

*Round mound weep wilt
Puss thrust through rash skins brims eruption
The body battles deep inside
This possessed, possessing, suckling malady
As life is life to propagate?
And death must survive, live?
Host, spread a cast bacteria
Diphtheria or Malaria.*

*Times scabs scab crusty ashes scars from wars
The battle done, won or lost
Time to count the countless cost.*

*Four families remain from twenty-four
Left to care for children, hungry and poor
Twenty-six orphans with tears last lost drips drop onto rocks
Taste the stacs Styx salt kiss dismiss
For busy be to stay so still
When all around is chaos
Thank you Thanatos
The brother of Hypnos.*

Marooned on Stac an Armin 1728 (May 16th)

Through the silence
Cut glass dappled oars pat rings
The sun shine mock bleak black crude mood
As three men and eight boys return
To learn how swift Death's Angel
May harvest crops, locusts drops
Some archetypal plan so grand
Wastelands scabs own demand.

Marooned through winter on Stac an Armin
Left in awe. What? When? Some lie?
Eating raw eggs and old dried meat
Not knowing the reason why.

On a bleak black stac
The bothy rests
300 feet above the sea
Still there!
A feat to see,
Where eleven sat while winter spat
Snows hails rains jubilee.

Returning home...... home?
Gone to graves mass massed
94 lain to rest, no coffins
For what could wood would hide or save preserve
For the peat brown earth list lisp
A soul's last words.
Death's kiss.

Within the old man's crown
Another lowly grave's trench cut frown
Dug down deep burrows scalp to scar
Brows brow creased, perplexed, bewilderment
Indifferent
Stay safe stacs moulded claws
As life and death compete
Preamble wrangle trample tangle chipping flaws
Delete.

Heersht...... Heersht...... Heersht

Feelings of unease, within the calm, a tension
The whisper from the waves is.....somehow.....uneasy
The whispering voices are....louder....more hurried
GO NOW! Reader if you wish
For I know not what waits for us
Be tales tells spells
Or minds torturous trapped nightmares
QUICKLY GO!
I shake my head to wakkeeeeeeee.......

I find myself standing at the entrance to a cave
There are thousands of deaths dying screams
I cover my ears
Yet the sounds of spirits creep through my clawing trembling fingers.
I am living in a nightmare and I cannot escape.
I walk into the cave for I know
To run will be to no avail.

Suddenly I see a figure sitting in the shadows sobbing
I KNOW THIS FACE!
'Tis the face from 'Kildun House' on the Isle of Lewis.*

I scream 'Stop the noise! Stop the noise!'
Yet dying souls trapped on no mans land
Fall down an everlasting divide
Between life and death
For who may dare
May not always win
So easy life to give or take
Only the gods play games
Upon the chequered board of Fate.

* *(Poetic Tales from the Isle of Lewis)*

Bonnie Prince Charlie 1746 (April)

In a tall stac's cave
Way down low sat the forlorn prince
As he held his head and cried
For dreams and fortune never wait
Be the devil turn up late.

Several days past since Culloden Moor
Blood flowed, staining clothes and blades
Brave warriors cries from victories
Far cry from the deep dug graves.

"My head! My head! The screams will not leave my mind
Echoes bouncing in my ears
Spirits that haunt me, time after time.

AHHHHHHHHHHHHHHHHH NO! NO! NO MORE!"

The light from the cave's opening was suddenly covered by the silhouette of a woman's slender shadow, her hair was Red and wild and flayed.

Lady Grange *and* **Bonnie Prince Charlie**

Lady Grange	Bonnie Prince Charlie
Charles Edward Stuart!	Lady Grange!
What have you done?	But! You died last year on Skye
I wait for the Wordcatcher	Even you come to haunt me
You will haunt yourself	To pick at my rotting bones
And live in hell	For there is no escape for me
I told you what I saw	Your dreams
NO! Your nightmares	Wars cannot wait for seers
And now the dead wait forever	KILL ME! KILL ME!
You will die every day	One bit at a time
I TOLD YOU! I TOLD YOU!	BITCH!
And you banished my truth	NOW! God is punishing me
By answering your prayers	NO! My prayers were to win
NO! Your dreams were to be king	I...I...am a pretender
Please do not feel sorry for yourself	Cheaters never win
And winners never cheat	GO AWAY!
NO!	WHY?

I wait for the Wordcatcher
He is here now
To release my pain
If you are happy
And if you are unhappy
I feel love for you
Love is
Whatever another
My torment is now at rest
I told you what I saw
Yes, in my dreams
Yes, and for the truth
Locked away
I sat in a dungeon
For I had seen
Thousands of deaths
AH! Pass the blame
And I told you
Youth deceives us all
Better to die on your feet
Now you must live with your mistake
At the edge of the world
AH! All Kings who lead thousands
And all Kings make mistakes
AH! The easy way out
Yet I did
I was left on this Island
And you are seeing yourself
Do as I did, sleep through the day
NO! At night the dreams will come
Now I am free
Now I am free
I bear no ill will anymore
You have been young
GOOD BYE
Remember, love will free you
GOOD
BYEEEEEEEEEEEEEEEEEEEEEEEEEEEE............................

The Devil, a Witch
AH! To Tell Tales
AH! Release me?
Time will last for seconds?
NO! Time will last forever
How? Why?
Loving?
Becomes?
While mine begins
In your dreams
You saw the future
You were punished
Hidden
NO! NO!
The truth which hurts
It was the English and the French
They said they would meet with us
The truth, and I was deceived
Yet thousands died
Than to live on your knees
Where am I?
And alone
Are alone
Please.....Let me die?
I cannot carry this burden
You knew the truth!
This place is as a mirror
Please! What will I do?
AH! Because I am hunted?
AH! NO! You float away!
And I am a prisoner within myself
Forgive me, PLEASE?
What have I done?
Pretender
NO! Do not leave me
PLEASE STAY!

Heersht......Heersht......Heersht
Calm today, peaceful,
The waves whisper as if weary
Resst......Resst......Rest
Mists play wisps teasing breeze
Peace again
I close my eyes to return to sleeps calm bliss
Some divide between sleep and dreams
Tranquillity sleeppppppppp

AHHHHHHHHHHHHHHHH!

My pounding heart so safe at home
Beats burst cursed caged to escape
NO! NO!
Three ships dive through the mists
100 'Red Coats' charging onto 'Village Bay'

The Hunting of the Prince 1746 (June 20°)

The 'Furnace' The 'Looe' and The 'Terror'
Rumble grumble trembling shores to thunder
100 'Red Coat' Soldiers, charging forth to plunder.
General Campbell

"Quickly! Men, run to search the houses, catch those people trying to escape. Prepare row boats and crews to search the shores and caves".

Two young soldiers approach the houses hoping for some ale or fresh meat, tae wash away the taste of dry biscuits. "*Phew! These houses stink, OOOOR AAAH* I've been sick, look at the dung on the floor, an' dead birds".

"Let's get out o' here, the floor must be two foot deep in muck".

General Campbell shouted orders to the boat crews "Row around the island, search the caves and leave no stone unturned, and let us be done and away from this cussed place".

*The men rowed hard and fast
For something in the air
Within the mind
Quick thoughts could not surpass.*

*Between the stacs of Boreray
A deep dark cave was seen
And each man looked the other way
So none would know what's been
And no man shouted out a name
So none would take the blame.*

*From the cave's deep depths came haunting sounds
For to chill each soldier's spine
For within their minds all could hear
Echoes from wars sad cries of fear
And each man looked the other way
So none would know what's been
And no man shouted out a name
So none would take the blame.*

*In the cave's dark arch
Swirl ghostly mists
Which all the soldiers seem to miss
And each man looked the other way
So none would know what's been
And no man shouted out a name
So none would take the blame.*

Homeward Bound

*Three ships set sail into the night
Within a silence of bewilderment
And General Campbell screamed aloud,*

*"What be with you men
such silence I have never afore known".*

*And each man looked the other way
So none would know what's been
And no man shouted out a name
So none would take the blame.*

1799

Laird of Islay *and* Marion Gillies

Your hair so fair and long	My Laird you flatter me
Your eyes, blue as the sky above	My Laird you make me blush
Your skin as soft as the silk of love	My Laird you must not touch
Your lips as sweet as grapes	Your kiss is very rough
You are a pearl	OH! Your hand!
While the island is your oyster	You should not touch
My mind is in a whirl	I am an innocent girl
My love for you is like no other	Then you will wait my lover
I will wait until the stacs fall down	And the sky falls to the earth
So marry me my own fair maid	OH! Robert you are so bold
My love is true please, marry me?	On your return you will be told
Marion Gilles! Please marry me?	Upon your return
I beg of you	I will tell you then.

Cambell's ship set sail to sea
To the fair isle of Islay
And he dreamed dream's dreams of what could be
Of Marion so beautiful
Upon the island of the free.

Time fly by, and he did return
And he let the cannons blast
To celebrate
Love's golden gate
True love
Within the hand of fate.

The islanders ran to hide
From the cannons terrified
And with the people gone
There was no one
And no fair blushing bride.

Cambell and his men
Searched and searched
But not one person could they find
So in the end, his ghost remained to cry
Be the chance of love
Passed by.

Marion's Lament

As Robert Cambell's galley
Sailed home to the Isle Islay
The night was dark
And the stars beamed twinkling bright
And the moon flicked waves
Washed sparkling stardust light

'My Laird of love, I do love you
And my heart will always sigh
For when I look into your eyes
True love can never die'.

And as he cried for his lost bride
The whispering breeze did sigh
For a sad lament is oft times sent
As a tear drop passes by.

Please note; the following lament
Is from Marion Gillies
(Scots Magazine 1802/18)

I love the youth whose locks are brown
Great is the love I bear to him
I gave him a kiss in the evening; Ah! How he then embraced me
Happy indeed was our meeting
Though revilers make free with our fame
It is wonderful that I should rejoice?
Good caus have I to be gay
Since first the youth beheld me
Since the day he gave me his heart
And promised his faithful love
His ribbands stream on my shoulders
They brightly encircle my head, and bind in ringlets my hair.

I detest them who harken, I hate all who listen and tell
They delight to defame, Scandal is forever their theme
Were I blest with the power of writing
I would soon send to – a letter
To tell my love of my state
And inform him how every tongue speaks
To his undoing and mine.

With thee I would fly through the world
When shall I hear from my love?
When will he run to my arms?
Though I had for my portion all the riches
Possessed by the wealthy son of Bernera
I could yield it all for thee and be happy
I would yield it my dear, to live with thee in a desert
Where no step could approach us
And no voice of man could be heard.

Though I delight to be merry
I will henceforth shun the young men
He who has wooed and won me; to him I will be faithful
I will not join their follies–no more rejoice in their sports
Angus descended from the tribe of Gillies
Angus of the dark brown locks, once I was thought to be thine
Nor did I spurn at thy suit
But he, my beloved, came from his Isle
I will listen no more to thy voice.

The Apostle of the North 1822 (September 16th)

Reverend John MacDonald
The 'Wild Man of Ferintosh'
Evangelist zealous preacher
One more who knows the 'way to be'
God's own righteous teacher.

Buchen's old manse gone now
Faiths lost hope
No church or chapel
Just a simple barn for prayers to pray
As where Jesus was born, or
Be the closer to God
The more you pay?

No gaiety dancing or wine 'Tis wrong'
NO MORE! NO MORE! The love of song
A religious orthodoxy and ideology
The nature of the people begins to change
No more jesting joviality.

The fatalist's fatalism brings fatal fatality
For who can weep
Down a one-way street
With no hope or destiny.

1827 The new church and manse are built
By stone masons from Dunvegan
Designed by Robert Louis Stevenson
An antithesis for the pagan.

And the manse was joined onto the church
Be the weathers storm or hail
For the minister shall have his way
And the Good Lord will prevail.

Reverend John MacDonald's
Last visit was in 1830
For the Lord moves in mysterious ways
His calling forth
To the grave byways.

Heersht......Heersht......Heersht

Standing solemn listening to the listless waves
Depression, grey clouds heavy
For changes made will stay
As laughter fades away.

I cannot seem to leave this spot
Each night......the same sad feeling.

I remember the beginning
When the people were relaxed and happy,
Before the rules.

The people are vulnerable to superstition
They believe everything which is told them
They do not seem to realize that being separated
From society they may have developed a utopia
A utopia which is now being eaten away.

I wake to write....
I have no feelings to express....
Is this...

THE END

Heersht......Heersht......Heersht
Standing solemn listening to the listless waves
Depression, grey clouds heavy
For changes made will stay
As laughter fades away.

The Great Auk

"*Hello...Hello...Sir, can you help me?*"
I looked behind me, and there, standing facing me, was a young boy who was about ten years of age. "*You...You can see me?*"

The boy shouted back as if I was silly, "*OF COURSE I CAN SEE YOU; you are standing right in front of me!*" He continued to shout at me as if I was 'hard of hearing', "*Have you seen any Auks? They seem to have disappeared? Have you seen any?*"

"*No...No I think they may be extinct*".

The boy puffed his cheeks full of air and placed his hands onto his hips, "*OH! What do you mean 'xtink'?*"

"*I mean that, I think they have all been eaten*".

The young boy seemed agitated, "*Well! There must be one left somewhere, I will save the last one!*"

As he started to walk away, the boy reached for my arm, but his hand passed through my image, "*OH! What was that! Are you a ghost?*"

"*No, I am asleep at home and dreaming*".

The boy's face instantly changed to an expression of twisted perplexity. Just as quickly, his face returned to an expression of excitement which reflected the importance of his mission. He continued to shout orders and assume command, "*Well! Follow me! And if you see an Auk, shout, 'AUK'*".

I followed the boy, for what else had I to do all night? I was curious, how could the boy see me? The only person to see me before was Lady Grange who had died on the 'Isle of Skye'. As I followed the boy, I watched in amazement as he climbed the rocks and stacs. I decided to ask the boy his name, "*What is your name?*"

"*My name is Finlay MacQueen, what is your name?*"
"*My name is Colin Demét*".
"*That's a funny name 'Colin Dimit'*".
"*It is a French name pronounced Demay*".
"*What's French mean?*"

"France is another country".
"AH! Past Long Island".
"Yes".

We searched the island for Auk's but could not find any. Each night for many nights, as I would stand upon the beach and stare out at the gloomy sea, the boy, Finlay would appear. I would always hear him before I could see him, *"AH! Colin! Quickly! Come follow me, we must find an Auk!"*

I was curious as to the intention of my encounters with the boy. Was there some message being given to me? Was I to carry on my writing of the tales from St. Kilda, from here? I decided to write what I could see, for there was nought else I could do.

"COLIN....COLIN"

"You do not have to shout Finlay, I can hear you".

"Well! You seemed miles away, dreaming, you are always dreaming. NOW! Come, let us find an Auk!"

"Tell me Finlay, why do you search for an Auk?"

"I search to save the Auk.. I must make sure the last one survives".

After many nights spent searching, Finlay found his elusive Auk. There, sat calmly on a ledge was the magnificent Great Auk. While searching for the bird, Finlay had told me of the creature's vulnerability. He had told me how the proud bird would sit calmly while the cragsman's noose was slipped over its head as it was hunted. Finlay told me how the Great Auk would only lay one egg which was another reason why the bird had vanished.

Finlay climbed to the ledge where the mighty Auk was sitting. What was he going to do? I felt the grey clouds approaching; I felt the sadness I had known when I was standing by the sea.

"FINLAY! What are you doing?

"SHHH, you will frighten the Auk".

Finlay carefully lifted the bird, which must have been about three foot tall, from the ledge. The Great Auk let out an awesome screech, as Finlay threw the bird into the air. The Auk flew downwards as it dived into the deep green sea. Finlay had told me how the Auk was not very good at flying; like a Penguin, the Auk was more at home in the water.

Finlay reached forward and took the last Auk's egg.

"NO! FINLAY! What are you doing?"
I watched in horror as Finlay placed the Auk's egg into a bag which was hanging from his waist.
"Don't worry Colin, I will not fall and break the egg".
"You must put the egg back; it may be the last one".
"It is the last one; the last one must be saved!"
Finlay climbed down from the rocks and started to walk towards the village.
"Finlay, if the egg hatches the chick will die without its mother".
"I am the bird's last hope, have they not all been lost?
"But, Finlay, that was because of people taking them".
"Well Colin, I promise you no-one will take this one".
I tried to take the bag which was holding the egg from Finlay, yet my hand passed through.

Finlay would not listen to reason and who was I to try to change the hand of fate, for who-so-ever alters past regrets, plays God, for to pay the following day.

I watched the next day, and the next. Finlay had placed the egg into an old bird's nest which he kept next to the peat fire at his home. An old wooden cross stood next to the egg and Finlay prayed every hour for the salvation of the bird.

"Lord God in heaven please save this bird from the hand of man, Amen".

One day when I arrived at Finlay's house the egg had hatched. The scrawny fledgling was almost dead. There was the occasional movement from its tiny beak. Finlay prayed and tried to feed the chick from food which he had chewed in his mouth. Unfortunately the last Great Auk died and with tears in his eyes, Finlay looked at me and asked a question, "*Colin, people have killed all the Auks. Why is it that God would not save the last one?*"

Before I had time to think of a possible answer for my friend, I was spun around, to suddenly find myself standing back on the beach. The grey clouds had disappeared and the sea began to whisper waves lost tales.

I had no answer for Finlay, I only had a need to write. I woke up at home. I rushed from my bed to my desk, to continue with my tales.

Reverend Neil MacKenzie 1829

"I will save your souls from extinction"
Resident minister to St. Kilda
Brought up at Glen Sannox
By the 'Sound of Bute'
Where the 'Holy Island'
As a footprint
Steps to the Isle of Arran
One tread, frozen, tribute.
Ministering to the peoples needs
With his bride from Glasgow
And six hungry children's mouths to feed.

Cleanliness and Godliness
Homes and land
All put to rights
For everything should have its place
As the daytime follows night
Or....Night-time follows day?
For the circle spin as the day begin
For another endless plight.

New houses with clean floors
And locks upon the doors
New dykes for cattle
On the fields to roam
No more to rest at home.

Reading the same newspapers
Each day's one from last year
For tomorrow's news
Repeats reviews
For time's own feat is an endless beat
In a lonely village street.

1844 Neil MacKenzie
Was sent to Duror in Appin
All of God's work truly done
For a web laid egg
On a feather bed
Can never ever run.

Heersht......Heersht......Heersht
The waves are heavy and restless, pounding angrily
The rocks of time washed clean
The sunken barnacles always stick
Parasite suck strife
The flowing blood of life
Leach lean learn lain lame lone love
The dictators seal of blood.

Reverend John MacKay 1865

The old man's watch stopped years ago
For who needs time
With a bell to chime
Sunrise - Sunset days flow.

Twenty-four years of intolerable gloom
Be the clinking bell from the old church room
Flocks flock no hurry with sorrowful looks
Eyes to the ground without a sound.

Three services on a Sunday with no pews to sit to rest
Each lasting for three hours
New commandments for to save a soul be God's eternal test
From Saturday night 'til Monday morn
NO washing of the hands
NO talking or whistling
NO milking of the cows or ewes
NO water to be drawn
NO looking to the left or right
Be the sins of the devil
Who delight?

The precentor strikes a tuning fork
And all whine as if in the pain of hell
For where they are is all so far
From the dreams of the wishing well.

No children's books allowed
A bible underneath the arm
To recite the Lord's last psalm.

The Queen of St. Kilda

Anne MacDonald was a troublesome woman
Six feet tall with twisted looks
The devil's eye to terrify
Her look was the curse of luck.

MacKay's housekeeper, Anne was
A planter of discord
To scold and preach
And hiss through her teeth
Like a snake in a long grass wreath.

Elected 'The Queen of St. Kilda'
As bigoted as MacKay
With the power to rule
The two did drool
For control is the bully's lie.

Games and picture books
As a gift were not allowed
For to hide from facts
In the prison stacs
Brings a frown
To the old man's crown.

A stove was given to warm the church
Where the tiny children prayed
'Sacrilegious', Anne said, as she
Raved and raved and raved.

She insisted the stove be left to rust
In the porch of the old church manse
For comfort and joy and happiness
Best not be left to chance.

1889 October

Twenty-four years of misery
"I think it is time I was leaving them now!"
Old MacKay hobbled to his boat
To meet his Lord
In Heaven? Or in Hell?
Sigh the peel of the death watch bell.

Heersht......Heersht......Heersht
The silence screams with pain and emotion
The winds begin to rage with icy claws
My body, warm at home in the cottage
Yet such cold pain I have never known
I shiver uncontrollably
Ice is everywhere, the stacs are white, like demons bony talons
The streams and pools are frozen
Misty figures swirl dusty snow-flaked ghosts of ice
Invisible energy? Spirits?
Teasing snow-flakes dancing whispers kiss of?...of?
Death? I feel, NO! GO!
Are you still here.e.e Reader.r.r?
May be.e.e you.u.u should.d.d
Go.o.o.o.o.o.o.o.o.o.o.....

Lockjaw
Tetanus Infantum
The Sickness of Eight Days
Tiny coffins made before the birth
Born to die so young infant infantile
Eight days of life's own pain and strife
One lifetime's score paid in full, pass over
Legacy, sighs and sins and baby's whims
Must pay as all for all, for all we know
Defenceless innocence bequeath
Some hell bent twisted torture
Some past lived sinner's sin
As soon as born beginning
Some mistake on earth
Forgiveness for a fool
The hand of God will
Must rule control
For the coffin is
Always open.

On the sixth day their suckling stopped
The milk of life and love.
On the seventh day their jaws locked
Gums clenched together tight
Nothing taken from above
On the eighth day convulsive fits
As if possessed, their strength
Drained fighting something
For what do babies know of fighting death
Except to learn from life and love
And pain and hate for
Left or Right
Heaven or hell
The poet's romance to guess
While the preachers all foretell
Some unknown eternal quest.

INFANTILE TETANUS
1830–46 DEATHS INFANTS 32 Male   9 Female
1855–76   "   "   26 "   15 "
Approximately 8 out of 10 children died of tetanus at this time.
The population before the outbreak of tetanus was
approximately 100.
At least 82 infants died from the disease.

The Knee Woman
Dipped dabbed dabbled sloth
Fulmar oil and the dung's old cloth
In an old gannet's stomach
Where the oil was kept
The umbilical cord
Was wiped with death.

Heersht......Heersht......Heersht
*I walked along the beach towards Village Bay,
the sun was bright and the birds flew lazily around the stacs.
I could see the islanders standing along the beach,
they were excited, like children waiting for an important event,
They were wearing their best, 'Sunday clothes'.
The islanders started jumping, waving, and pointing
towards the oceans concave horizon where smoke puffs puffed
across a pale blue sky.
The ship's steam-engine pounded its pistons exploding relief
Like an old man, wearily shovelling coal*

Oooph... ah...Oooph...ah...Oooph...ahhh

*The Dunara Castle dropped anchor off shore
while several islanders rowed out to greet them.
The passengers were taken to shore for a
'Shilling a head'
The steamer season had begun, it was now the most important
time of the year for the occupants of St. Kilda.
The islanders had found their apple in their
'Garden of Eden'.*

DUNARA CASTLE
The Tourists 1877 (July 2ⁿᵈ)

The tourists were met by the island's women as they landed. They were greeted and given eggs and bunches of marigolds, white heather and other mementos. Tourists rarely spent more than half a day on the island. They stared in amazement at the beauty of the landscape, as they soaked in the atmosphere from the edge of the world.

I wondered if the old man would be amused by the strange strangers, walking around his crown, pointing and touching rocks and flowers. *NO?* He stands as he always has? Waiting, or ..... Nothing ...... A beginning for a monumental end.

For the sea was rising be the tide turn low.

GLASGOW AND THE HIGHLANDS.

TOUR TO ST. KILDA,

Via IONA, MULL, SKYE, and HARRIS.

THE splendid sea-going Steamer "DUNARA CASTLE" (having superior accommodation for Passengers), is intended, on her voyage to the West Highlands of 28th June, to call at the Island of ST. KILDA.

The Steamer will leave GLASGOW on THURSDAY, 28th June, at 2 p.m., and from GREENOCK at 7 p.m., arrive at St. Kilda early on Monday morning, when, weather permitting, Passengers will have several hours ashore. If too stormy to land, the Steamer will sail round the Island, and then return, *via* Sound of Harris and usual ports of call, to Glasgow, arriving there on the following Wednesday night.

FARE to ST. KILDA and Back, £5.

Berths may be secured on application to

MARTIN ORME,
20 ROBERTSON STREET.

GLASGOW, *May 10, 1877.*

"Souvenirs....Souvenirs"
Sheepskins, wool, tweed, scarves,
Fulmar wings and gannets beaks
Blown birds' eggs sold upon the beach
Old spindles, clothes and brooches
Querns, no qualms to cross wet palms.

'Lick the Pennies' 'Penny Lickers'
While the tourists laugh and sigh
Flicking toffees toffee wrappers
Collecting coins bye the bye.

Pennies from heaven
Laughing at them, as they pray in church
Crooning and crowing the sacred word
Photographs will cost to price
As the cragsmen climb
Pennies fall for the risk of life.

The apple plucked and bitten must be eaten
For soon be rotten to the core
And one sweet bite, to kiss dour lips
The devil always calls for more.

For the need of greed is a mouth to feed
And like the leach will bleed and bleed
For the more to seed is a law decreed
Discussed disgusts lust's mislaid mistrust
Heed creed deals deed greed's greed.

The malign and cumulative influence of tourism, religion and disease; the lack of demand for the produce from St. Kilda; the growing dependence on charity and increased feelings of greed for modern commodities from the outside world began to cause feelings of discontentment amongst the islanders.

    The people who once lived in peace and worked together as a community, became divided by strife and feuds.

A microcosmic reflection from the rest of the world?
Peace and calm, to war and hate from the recipe of...Desire?
Has the old man always known the answer?
Ask for nothing and do not force others to follow your ways.

Heersht......Heersht......Heersht
It's wonderful today!
YEPEE......YEPEE
I dance and sing and spin
For birds are singing once again
Grey clouds are gone
Sweet rainbows mandolin
YEPEEDY......DOO-DA
The sun is shining brightly
While the moon is smiling in the sky
And a mocking bird flies by.

1890
The Marriage of
Annie Ferguson to **Neil Gillies**

The new 'Queen of St. Kilda'	I love you true
From birth always	Our love has been
Always forever	And always will be, forever
True love will be	Our first kiss will never die
For in your eyes	I see the freedom of
The seas deep depths	Everlasting love
Swirling caressing moist	With open lips
The deepest kiss	I submit, my all for you
Suckle my breasts	My love
For an eternity	Always
Always together	In a circle
In a golden hue my love	One ring so true.

True Loves
White doves fly free
For the Queen of all beauty
Your long white dress adorned
With primrose yellow flowers, rings your crown's sweet perfume
The old man's stacs bow down to peep
As rainbows arch leap golden treasure
Safe bequeathed beneath.

People travel from distant lands
With hopes of seeing love
For dreamers dream's dream endlessly
Always somewhere so far away
For over seas and distant lands
The edge of the world
Holds dreams
Yet a gift of gold
Cannot but hold
Moonbeams!
Cannot be sold.

Phantasmagoria
From Sunderland in Yorkshire.
Form a queue, Ian Campbell's tour with wedding gifts
Porkie pies and Bovril some Digestive syrup
A dress for the bride and a wedding cake
A tangle of old spectacles and some old books
Be the gate crash bash
Mistake.

Turned away at the sea-side Quay
From dreams of loves own show
For who may catch the snowflake's cast
In a hand's fist the palm sweat flow.

And as the ship did sail away
Sad faces stared in awe
From a quarter deck
With a craning neck
Back to Yorkshire's grass groan grown moors more.

And the tallest stacks began to laugh
At the syrup and the tangled glasses
For a price to pay
To capture love
From a land so far away.

In the church by the manse
The two knelt low
And bowed their heads to God
To be blessed with love and faith and hope
With a bond from the Lord above.

In the lines of pews
Some people sighed
While others happily
Cried and cried
For love can rise to touch the wise
And the meek will kiss your cheek
A simple line may outlast time
On the isle of the pointing peak.

The bond be made forever more
As the celebrations begin
For the people laugh and dance and sing
Whilst the youngsters spin and spin.

Drinking wine
In a dancing line
Be a tap toed turn to do
All turn left and all turn right
Going under 'dootsey woo'.

Dancing around
The old man's stacs
As the shadows weave and wave
The old man's head vibrates with joy
For the happy
Girl and Boy.

Followed to the warm bed room
Be the giggles laughs and sighs
For all know who what lovers do
When true hearts meet
Inside.

The Mini Mail Boats

'St. Kilda Mail Please Open'

Tiny Mail Boats sailing, far across the sea
Will you send one now for me?
In a little boat with a crumpled note, to sail
Battling on through the howling wind and hail.

Lady Grange's messages were the first mail boats
Pieces of cork tied tight with yarn to yarn
For Edinburgh for to sail
All so far across the sea
The prisoner's trembling mail.

Shipwrecked sailors
Tiny model boats with sails
Bouncing o'er the mighty waves
Burnt to brand upon the deck
OPEN THIS
Trapped men's hope
Of the lands they miss.

1885
A message in a bottle
In a tiny boat's hold hatch
Three foot long, be a yard arm strong
With a sail and a hull with an iron weight
To be launched to the hand of fate.

1900s
Send a message for £1
To float with hope across the sea
For who may catch a fleeting glance
Of a chance of mystery.

Be love or treasures dreams in a tiny boat
Or a simple message forever lost
And sailing still
Afloat.

Hunger 1912

Bitter winter winds, snows blanket cringe
No mail. No supplies,
Roar the creeping beating tide
In the white topped houses
Dug in deep
From the rain and hail and sleet.

Gail's hound sound round hunting
Cracks and crannies
Testing tied roofs aloof
Rip, tear relentless
Stacs the edge of time
All hell let loose
Around each stac and home
The devil's tied tried plied noose.

Dried birds and eggs
From the frozen cleits
No food for the cattle, chickens, sheep,
As one by one the beasts bleed dry
For the stew to skew
Keep the peat fires high.

On and on until May, may be an end
When a fishing boat meets need to feed
The Islanders starvation
Lost hope last breath bequeathed.

H.M.S. Achilles
Supplies, supplies of food and clothes
To a beaten battered weary folk
On the island at the edge
Of the world
Be the war of the ice fires smoke.

Influenza Epidemic 1913

*Another winter to weather wither
Snow and ice and burley winds
AH! At rest this year
Weary from the fear of fear.*

*And yet the storm does have an eye
Only the fool does rest to watch contentment
For by the by
The stacs stakes high
And in the devil's game
Death's dead souls wait
In a line of endless pain.*

*One visit from a distant friend
One germ, germinate, create to liquidate
The lungs coughs spit
The nose drips drips
Sweat blood and tears
Welcome to the world
A world without stacs tiers.*

*But one more nail in a coffins lid
Sometimes luck's fortune turn
Be a one way trip
In the devil's quip
No help
With a stone hand's quern.*

*For several months
The virus jump
Before medical aid arrived
For another year with a life of fear
And an end
Fate's hand adheres.*

Heersht...... Heersht...... Heersht
The water is like glass today
No ripples.
The towering stacs reflections lie, to lie? Upon the oceans skin
And with the gentle swell
They seem to sway as if to dance
Some taunting haunting seductive......
AAAHHHHH!
From the water, diving out, some phallic symbol?
NO! A German submarine, like some giant rising whale
Towering tall against the pale blue sky
I quickly rub my eyes, is it a whale?
NO! The submarine crashes down to smash the glass of the sea
Exploding white-washed waves of thunder
Guns fire echoing through the trembling stacs
One blast sounding like twenty
NO! The island's tiny store has been hit by a shell.

AH! The old man's crown meets modern war
For the end is always the same
One common denominator, dominator
Destruction.

War 1914
A British Naval Base
Stationed on the island
Provides a vital link of regular supplies
And communications from naval supply vessels.
Five years of settled change
Can the pasts lost ghosts remain?
Or, for worse, or for better return?

Can the grains flow back
Within the hour glass
OH! Turn and start again?
1919
The Naval detachment was withdrawn.

THE PETITION *1930 (May 10ᵗʰ)*

I Reverend Dugald Munro, and I Williamina Barclay being the resident nurse upon St. Kilda, hereby bear witness to the signing of the aforesaid petition of evacuation from the island of St. Kilda by all Householders, Widows and every person of a working age.

We the undersigned the natives of St. Kilda hereby respectfully pray and petition Her Majesty's Government to assist us all to leave the island this year and to find homes and occupations for us on the mainland... We do not ask to be settled together as a separate community, but in the meantime we would well and truly be very grateful of assistance and transference elsewhere where there would be a better opportunity of securing our livelihood.

Heersht......Heersht......Heersht

Another peaceful day at Village Bay
I look along the row of houses
A breeze blows miniature tornadoes down the dusty road
I am reminded of the old western films I have watched on T.V.
I am frightened, of the silence and peace of St. Kilda
For the storm always seems to follow the calm.
There is a ghostly silence
I look around myself
The towering pinnacles are adorned with fluffy clouds
Which float around the stacs
As each one turns individually
Like mandarins harlequins dancing to mandolins.

I begin to walk, cautiously along the road.
OH! The door from a house slowly opens
I walk into house No.2.
For I now realise what I am meant to do.

The Last People *from the* Edge of the World
Village Bay 1930 June
House No2

I slowly walk through the open door. The cottage is dark with shadows, shades flickering around the room.

A tall elderly man is standing facing me. His beard is long and black and he is wearing a flat topped hat. With a booming voice which startles me, he began to laugh, *"HA HA HAR! It is you! My friend Colin Dimmit!"*

I was lost to wonder, *"Who.... Who....are you?"*

"Do you not remember me Colin? FINLAY...FINLAY MacQUEEN HA HA HAR"

Now I remember, *"AHH! Finlay, the boy who found the last Auk's egg".*

"HA HAR, you remember me Colin, and do you remember my question?"

"I...I...Think it was something about all the Auk's dying".

"My question Colin, was, 'People have killed all the Auks.

Why is it that God would not save the last one?"

"I....I am sorry Finlay, but I am not a philosopher".

"And what are you, spirit, for I am a seer and can see you?"

"I see things when I am asleep and I awake with the words in my minds eye to save"

"AH! Colin, you are a seer?

"The people I meet in dreams call me 'The Wordcatcher'"

"AH! Colin the Wordcatcher, YES! I like that name".

"Well Finlay, it is easier to say than Demét".

Finlay MacQueen filled the room with his booming laughter, as his hat fell to the floor from the jerking of his body, *"HA HA HAAAR HAAR, Dimit, Demit, Damit. Aye, I will call you Colin!"* Finlay opened a cupboard door and lifted out a mighty Auk, a mighty STUFFED AUK, *"This is the last Auk, and YES! It was saved forever, by me".*

Finlay pushed the dead bird towards me with an expression of pride and achievement beaming from his face. The bird was stiff looking. My mind moved; flicking between the comprehension of the bird being alive and dead. The creature bore the nature of horror, and its smell was the smell of death. I did not wish to offend Finlay, as all in all, what was done was done. *"Well done Finlay, tell me, my friend, how old are you now?*

"I am 68 years of age and still able to climb the stacs and I am the best cragsman in the world. Now Colin! Look at the other birds I have saved".

Finlay proceeded to show me his collection of stuffed birds. Eventually he offered me a Puffin which I reluctantly accepted. Fortunately my hands passed through the bird. I sighed with relief though I portrayed to Finlay an expression of disappointment. *"OH! Thank you Finlay, OH NO! My hands have passed through it".*

"ARR! You must not be sad Colin, you cannot have everything in this life you know!"

"Ah well, maybe in another lifetime Finlay my friend".

"Now! Colin, I have been asked to offer you my help".

"And who has asked you to help me Finlay?"

"It was the ghost of the earth-bound spirit of pain. She roamed the Isle like a ghost with a face from pain as such I have never seen, nor wish to again".

"Ah! Lady Grange, she is free now from her chains!"
Finlay looked frightened, and made a quick fleeting glance to his rear. He reached towards a small dish and quickly threw a pinch of salt over his shoulder, *"I was terrified of her when I was a child. I would see her ghost floating in the mists and one time I came face to face with her, and...and my heart stopped and I believed my time had come. Such pain as was in her eyes I have never seen before. A few weeks past, I saw her shape floating towards me. I will tell you now Colin, such fear I have never known, and yet, when she came close, she was beautiful and peaceful. She stared into my eyes and spoke to me softly. She said, 'Have no fear for I am free from pain and I mean you no harm. Please help my friend the Wordcatcher if needs be, for you are a seer and may see him', and then off she flies in a cloud and a wisp to vanish into the bright blue sky".*

"She is at rest now Finlay, and may God Bless her".

"Who was she Wordcatcher?"

"She was Lady Grange who was a prisoner on Kilda for seven years. I first saw her when I was visiting the Isle of Skye, and I wrote of her then. I...I...Think I can remember the verse:

January 22nd 1732.
She was taken in the dead of night
From the depths of Edinburgh
A hood tight and black upon her head
Be the cuss of a spy's last dread.

Imprisoned in Tyrim castle
By the Clanranald's of Moidart,
Then two years on a lonely isle, Heiskar,
A lonely twinkling, flickering star.

Seven years on St. Kilda
No companions, without friends,
I often wondered what the crime
So much unkind lost time.

Ten years of lonely living hell
Shipped to Assynt and then to Skye
To be hidden in a hidden cave
The Lady's living grave.

*She wandered Skye as a broken soul
Until death's grant to ease
For she died in 1745, from misery and disease.*

*Misery, disease and death
Buried at old Trumpan head
In an empty grave?
What prayers be said?*

*Many times return Wordcatcher
So sad, to help, to know,
Yet nothing in the eyes was seen
The barren flowers glow.*

*Sometimes shadows passed by
Memories lost floating, brief,
A wind to blow lost green dreams
The breeze blown crisp brown leaf".*

Finlay looked sad as he spoke, *"I remember the tales of Lady Grange, and the house she stayed in, sad....sad story".*

"And a long story Finlay, she was a woman who suffered for the sins of men and war. Now I must move on, for my nights are short and time is forever".

"How may I be of help to you Colin?"
"Walk with me through the houses and talk to the people, so I may catch the words".

"HAA HAA HAAR! Yes...Yes... Follow me Wordcatcher so that all will know, and all will know of Finlay MacQueen who saved the last Great Auk. Come with me my friend"

House No 1

"This is the home of the MacKinnons, the largest family on St. Kilda. Here lives Norman who is 50 years of age and his wife Annie of 42 years; she is the daughter of Finlay Gillies of No.7. They have eight children, Norman 20 years, Donald Ewen 19 years, Finlay 16 years, John 10 years, Neil 4 years, Mary 5 years, Christine 9 years and Rachel who is at the age of 13 years. We will go inside now Colin and I will do the talking".

"Well, you will have to do the talking Finlay, they cannot

see or hear me".

Finlay knocked on the door and walked into the cottage. The room was full of life, children were playing and shouting. Mary and Christine were rocking a doll which was tucked into the blankets of a crib, *'Git tae sleep now baby',* Mary screamed, *"STOP SHOUTING Neil MacKinnon, you'll wake the baby".*

Norman, the father of the family was busy sowing clothes. As Finlay entered the room Norman stopped sowing to greet his friend, *"Ah! Hello there Finlay, how are ye young laddy?"*

"I'm fit tae climb stac Lee laddy, and how's the finest tailor on the island and his beautiful wife?"

"We thank God for our health and the food we have tae eat"

"'Amen' Norman and I must say! Praise the Lord for the gift you have of the Precentor at the church services".

"'Amen' and I thank the Lord for the gift".

Finlay turned towards the mother of the family, Annie, *"How do you feel about moving from the island Annie".*

"Ahh! 'Tis sad...sad, but we have tae think of the children, there is nothing left for them here now. After last winter I promised the children we wouldnae stay for the next. Hunger is a terrible pain and tae see your young 'uns crying from the hunger is unbearable."

Norman continued to speak when Annie had finished, *"I will never forget when I was a wee laddy, and me daddy dancin' an' laughing an' shoutin' '1000 yards O' Tweed on order' an' every family had money in their pockets, most had £20 or more saved. I never would have believed it would a come tae this".* Looking sadly at the floor of the room, Norman continued, *"I dinnae know if I can live away from the island, yet I know we cannae live on it anymore. I dinnae want to need the island if I cannae live on it, that is all I know. There is nothing on the 'mainland' fir me, but I will go fir the children, we have nae choice now, after the last winter".*

Donald Ewen, who was 19 years of age, shouted, *"I wannie go tae the Black Isle and work on the fishing boats, I wannie be a sailor an travel the world tae see all them other countries an' places, an foreign peoples of different coloured skins".*

Finlay began to walk towards the door, *"Goodbye fir now and God bless yer home an all of ye".*

As we began to move from the room to leave the house of the MacKinnons, I noticed the youngest boy, Neil who was 4 years of age pointing and reaching out to me. When we had left the house and closed the door Finlay looked at me and said,

"Wee Neil could see ye Colin, HA HA! The wee laddy's a seer".

House No 2
"As ye know Colin, this is my house. I live here with my son Donald. My loving wife Mary, nee MacKinnon has passed over to heaven where she waits for me, 'God bless' her soul. My daughter Mary Annie was married to young Neil Ferguson, junior. My daughter Annie married Donald Gillies who lived at No.13".

House No 3
"This house is empty Colin. The Family of the MacDonalds had lived here since 1753. William MacDonald was a taxidermist and sold his birds to Manchester Museum. He was also the Precentor for the church until leaving the island. William MacDonald was the first person to move from the island and he took all his family with him in 1924. William MacDonald married Mary Ann MacQueen in 1895. William and Mary had 11 children, John, Finlay, Annabella, Mary, Mary Betsey, Finlay John, Callum, Kirsty, Rachel, Marion and Mae. William MacDonald's father who's name was Neil, married Isabella Ross Munro who was the servant of the Rev. John MacKay and his grandfather Callum married Betsy Scott, a mid-wife from Lochinver in 1834. Betsy Scott was the servant of the Rev. Neil MacKenzie".

House No 4
"This house is also empty. It was the home of Donald Ferguson who was the father of Alexander. Alex had become successful within the cloth trade in the city of Glasgow. He had a son Neil who became Postmaster on the island, Ah! And his daughter married John Gillies senior. Oh! And his other son became a missionary. NOW! Are ye taking in all o' this Colin?"

"Well! Could you repeat it all again please?"

"HA...HA...HA I tell ye it all again if ye have the time tae stay laddie, HA...HA...HA".

House No 5

"This is the home of Neil Ferguson senior who is married to Annie, my half sister. Their son Neil and his wife Mary Annie also live with them in this house and if we are to move soon from St. Kilda, Neil and Mary will be the last couple to have been married on the island. Neil senior is the Postmaster and also the School Manager. He also owns the Store and is the only Elder of the Kirk. Neil is also the Flockmaster and Ground Officer of the estate. I will knock to see if anyone is home".

Finlay knocked on the door and a voice from inside shouted, "*Come in*". I followed Finlay inside where a man of about 54 years of age was sat on a wooden chair reading a book. "*Hello Finlay! How are ye? Come on in man and take a wee seat*".

"*Thank ye Neil and God bless ye*". Finlay sat down on a chair next to Neil senior. "*Tell me Neil, what dae ye think about leavin' the island?*"

"*Ah away man, it be sad news, sad news, and so many of our people are obsessed with the mainland and Finlay*", Neil leaned over towards Finlay and whispered, "*Obsessions do not have reasons*".

Finlay spoke softly to Neil, "*What will you do if we leave the island my friend?*"

"*Ah! I have the chance of a job with the Forestry Commission on the Tulliallan Estate, there will be nothing left here to stay for*".

After a time we left Neil's house and we both felt deep feelings of sadness.

House No 6

We walked towards the next house, but as we approached the door, Finlay stopped, looked down at the ground with an air of sadness as he spoke,

"*This house we will not enter as it is a house of sadness. Angus Gillies and his loving wife Annie have both died in this house*".

We walked in silence to the next house. I felt uncomfortable. A deep sadness was growing as we visited each home. These were homes, not the empty shells which I knew they would soon become. I felt these were living homes which would soon die forever.

"*Hurry Colin, you haven't got all day, HA...HA...HA*"

House No 7

"In this house lives the oldest person on St. Kilda, his name is Finlay Gillies and he is 74 years of age. Finlay's wife, Catherine and their son Neil have passed away to heaven. Neil's widow Katie of 41 years also lives at this house with her two sons, Donald; 12 years old and Ewen whose 9".

Finlay knocked on the door which was opened by an elderly man wearing a cloth hat. The old man smiled through a white beard which reminded me of matted wool. His voice was high, and I sensed an aura of deep wisdom about this man. I longed to talk to him yet knew that was not possible. I followed Finlay into the home of Finlay Gillies and watched as the two men sat on wooden chairs by a wooden table. I prayed I would not wake up at this time. Finlay Gillies spoke softly, *"So it is my house now where you call Finlay. Ah! Something is afoot for I have seen ye walking down the row calling at every house, HA...HA...An' a talking tae yer self as well. I always said ye were away with the fairies".* Finlay Gillies knocked an old pipe onto the edge of the table before stuffing its bowl full of tobacco. *"Well! Finlay MacQueen, what are ye up to?"* Gillies stared unblinkingly and intently at MacQueen while belching clouds of smoke from his pipe.

"Ye dinnae miss much do ye Finlay Gillies? I'll be asking what people think about leaving the island is all".

"Well...Well Now! And who is it says anyone is leaving the isle?"

"The villagers I have spoken to are in a mind to move. They seem to be of the opinion that to stay now would be foolish".

Finlay Gillies puffed hard on his pipe, *"Foolish? Yes I suppose it would be foolish to try to beat the hand of fate. One day a thing is young, strong, and full of life, and then, within the changing of the tide, everything can change. When I was young there was contentment on the island, a contentment which has changed to greed. Now children cry for chocolate and toys, while their parents build dreams from visitors tales of gold and silver and wealth and power".*

Finlay MacQueen interrupted Gillies, *"I do not think the people want to leave, it seems as if the tide of change has moved for them".*

Gillies stared out of his home's tiny window as he spoke

slowly and sadly, "*Ay! The people are nae tae blame, for the hunger and illness has taken its lot. They have become dependent on the outside world and its charity, now they will not go back. Nae time will not turn backwards. The milk which has turned sour will not become whole again and the ice which melts and runs into the stream, then becomes a part of the ocean*".

Finlay MacQueen slowly rose from his chair by the table as he asked his friend Finlay, *"Will you leave the island? Where will it be you will go?"*

"Yes! I will leave St. Kilda, for I am old but not a fool. My heart will remain on the island as will my memories, loves and pains, and losses, for we must learn of loss before we can appreciate gain. I will finish my days thinking of my past at Lochaline. Now Finlay, I will leave you to your task, for it will not be long afore the row of our people has gone forever and tourists will stare and wonder into the empty shells of our homes".

Finlay Gillies walked to open his door, and as we were leaving, he asked, *"Are you to write a book my friend? Is that what you are doing?"*

Finlay MacQueen answered, "Y*es, all will be told",* and the door was gently closed.

We began to move towards the next house. I suddenly felt dizzy, as a familiar transgression began to interrupt my journey. I was waking up at home. I quickly shouted to Finlay, "I...I...Am beginning to wake up. Wait for me Finlayyyyyyyyyyyyyyyyyyyyyyyyyyyyyyyyyyyyyyyyyyyyyyyyyyyyyyyyyyyyyyy

"BUT, Colin! You were never asleep!"

*The Isle of Lewis 2006 (March 19*ᵗʰ*)*

I awoke at home in our old crofter's cottage by the sea. It was just becoming light and yellow streaks were brushed across the pale blue sky, as if the clouds had been wiped away to leave smears of golden honey.

A new day had begun and as usual my head was full of words. I clambered from the bed, slipped on my track-suit and rushed downstairs to write, leaving my wife Annette with peaceful dreams. I was immediately greeted by the whimpering of Amber our five month old Boarder Terrier puppy.

I glanced from my cottage window and **'WOW'** everywhere outside was covered in a thick blanket of snow.

"Quick Amber lets go and play!"

The front lawn was like a sheet of brilliant white paper, clean and pure, without a blemish. I walked into the snow which was about four inches deep. My feet made a crisp crunching sound. Amber dived into the snow which covered her legs as she tried to walk. She jumped and ran and bit the snow. I rolled snowballs and threw them for her. She barked and dived and ran free. Suddenly Annette, my wife, appeared awakened by the fuss. Snowballs were being thrown everywhere while Amber chased them trying to understand why they all disappeared when she bit them.

Eventually when we were all exhausted, Annette took Amber inside for her feed. I stared at the snow. It was amazing how one moment it was so pure and the next moment marred. I instantly felt sadness, for soon this snow would vanish, as if it had never existed.

I sat at my desk to write. My mind was full of the words from the people of Village Bay. I could not remember all of their names, or their ages. I searched through books for a record of the names and ages of the last people from St. Kilda.

I found all the names I had known.

"Ha! Finlay, I am back!"
"I had not noticed that you had been gone!"

House No 8

"This is the home of Callum MacDonald. He passed over to heaven recently. He was known as 'Old Blind Callum' and was loved by all. Old Blind Callum would take the church services in the absence of the Missionary and the Elder. He had been married twice. The first time to a cousin who was a MacDonald from No16. His second marriage was to Annie Gillies who was the daughter of Norman Gillies. Callum had one son, Donald and one daughter, Annie and they both have left St. Kilda".

Finlay leaned towards me and began to whisper,
while quickly glancing behind over his shoulders,
as if to see if someone was standing behind him.
He pressed one finger tightly onto his lips,

"Colin... Shhh!... Old Blind Callum was a 'seer'".

House No. 9

Finlay knocked upon the door of cottage No.9. There was no answer so Finlay opened the door and looked inside,

"They must be out, about there business Colin, so I will tell you who lives here, unless you want to come back?"

"I'm sorry Finlay, but I do not know if I will ever be back"

"Here is the home of J.R. MacDonald who is 59 years old; he is the son of William from No.3. He was away some years working on the drifters but returned to live here. Also living here is Annie Gillies; known as Mrs 'Scalpay' Gillies. Her husband Ewan died from a fall while climbing the crags beyond Mullach Mor. Annie's daughter, Mary Anne lives here too and she is 16 years old.

As we were walking away from MacDonald's home we were greeted by a pretty girl skipping down the road towards us. The girl was surrounded by barking dogs. Her face was beaming with the sunshine of happiness. She skipped and sang as the dogs barked all around her from excitement. She had a chain of flowers around her neck and carried a basket of large eggs. Finlay shouted to the happy girl, "Hello Mary Anne, you look happy as always!"

"Hello Finlay, I am happy, I will be going to the mainland soon and I will live in a beautiful home. I will find my truelove and be happy forever. I WANT TO GO NOW! I WANT TO GO NOW! I want to take all the dogs and....and.....I never want to eat another egg, and I never.....never.....ever want to eat another smelly bird".

Finlay waited until Mary Anne had stopped jumping and shouting, before trying to speak, "But Mary Anne what if the evacuation does not happen, remember, all the adults have to sign the agreement?"

"My mother will sign, and...and...Mr MacDonald said he will, if I stop bothering him and keep quiet,

HOORAY! HOORAY!
I'M GOING TO INVERNESS...S........I'M GOING TO INVERNESS...S"

Now, mixed with my feelings of sadness
Were also feelings of happiness
For from an end there is a new beginning
And from death an invitation of rebirth.

The snow was beginning to melt.

House No. 10
"This house is another empty house Colin. The owner is Donald MacQueen who moved to Glasgow several years ago".

House No. 11
Kirsty MacQueen who is of 59 years lives alone in this house; alone and in sorrow. Her husband Norman drowned with Lachlan MacDonald's father in a boating accident off Dun. Kirsty never had any children. Norman MacKinnon senior is her nephew. She is a widow who lives with sadness. I feel we should pass by her home".

"If you don't mind and Kirsty agrees, I would like to see her Finlay. If we do not visit her now, something may be lost forever".

Finlay had no need to knock on the door. He told me that Kirsty never answered the door. She never had much to say. Finlay said it was as if she was trapped in the past.

"HELLO KIRSTY, HOW ARE YOU?"

"There is nae need tae shout Finlay, I'll nae be deef yet".

"I have come tae see how ye are, and are ye looking forward tae moving tae the mainland?"

"I have nae desire tae stay or tae go, do as ye will".

AHHHHHHHHHHHHHHHHHHHHHHHHHHHHHHHHH!

Suddenly, there was a man's face, inches away from my own.
I was startled and shouted *"GO AWAY! GO AWAY!"*
Finlay shouted to me, *"What is wrong with you Colin?"*
Kirsty shouted to Finlay, *"Who is Colin?"*

The man moved to sit next to Kirsty by the fire side.

"What are you shouting for Colin?" Asked Finlay, whose white hair was now standing up straight, *"Ye scared the 'life out o' me'".*

"That man! That man! He scared the 'life out of me'".

"What man?" Asked Finlay, as he stared around the room.

Kirsty looked strangely at Finlay, *"Have ye gone completely mad man, standing there a talking tae yer self?"*

I began to realise that the man I could see, and Finlay

could not, was the spirit of Kirsty's husband Norman who had drowned. In some way which I do not understand, Norman may be some kind of 'earth-bound spirit' which may explain why Finlay could not see him.

I watched husband and wife sitting by the fireside as they held each the other's hand. They were snuggled closely together and there was a peace from their own contentment surrounding them.

I turned towards Finlay whispering, "*We must go now*".

Finlay whispered back to me, "I told you! Didn't I?"

House No. 12

"This was the home of Ewen Gillies, the son of Norman. He fell to meet with his fate whilst climbing the crags, and NO! I will not go into his home. His widow Annie and daughter Mary Anne 'whom you have seen' are now living at No.9.

House No. 13

Finlay knocked upon the door of the house and there was no reply. *"This is the home of Donald Gillies of 39 years. He is the son of John senior. Donald lives with his wife Christine, who is 35 years old, and their two daughters, Kathie 12 and Rachel 8 years of age".*

House No. 14

"This is the home of Mrs Annie Gillies of 41 years. Her husband Donald died of appendicitis whist on Boreray. She is left with two daughters, Rachel of 20 years and Flora of 11years. Annie's sister also died of T.B. last week. We should not enter their home as they are grieving for the loss of Mary. I can confirm that all the remaining family are of a mind to leave St. Kilda. Annie Gillies is of a firm belief that, if their family had been on the mainland her husband Donald would have been saved from his illness".

House No. 15

"Annie Gillies who is 65 years of age lives here. She is the Queen of St. Kilda and her loving husband Neil has passed away tae heaven"

"Sorry to interrupt you Finlay. I have seen the marriage of Annie and Neil".

"I know you have Colin! I was there. Remember? Annie's son John Gillies of 38 years also lives in the home, as well as John's son; Granny Gillies' grandson Norman of 6 years"

House No. 16

"This is the last home Colin. Rachel MacDonald lives here. She is a widow and is 67 years of age. Rachel lives here with her two sons, Ewen, 42 and Lachlan, 24. Rachel is a very kind woman; she has suffered the loss of her husband Donald in a boating accident off Dun. Yes! It was also the accident I told you about from home No.11, where Kirsty MacQueen's husband Norman also died. Rachel has also had the misfortune of her daughter Rachel passing to heaven. She has two other sons, Donald and Angus who have since moved to the mainland. From my conversations with Rachel, I know she is not of a mind to leave St. Kilda, especially now, as she is 67 years of age. She has said many times, 'I am too weary for long journeys and new beginnings'. Rachel will follow her family, as she could not bear to be parted from them all".

We stood in silence for a time. Finlay and I looked around St. Kilda. We stared at the towering stacs as if looking for answers to the riddles of time and fate. We could find no solution. Finlay looked at me and smiled. I could see the young boy again who once searched for the last Auk. I asked him,

"Where will you go Finlay my Friend?"

An expression of puzzlement crept over his face as he replied

"Where do you go from the edge of the world?"

Heersht......Heersht......Heersht
Gently the waves stroke the rocks and sand
As if to rush may wake to warn some secret stalking fate
For the wheel must turn and play the game
Delicately the delicacy deliberately debenture's debauchery
Sheep flock follow herd, heard
Less one escape
Agitate
And find some truths reflection.
Standing on the beach listening for the whispers
I quickly cover my ears for I hear the sounds of tears
Thousands of people sobbing
Heart rendering cries of torment and pain
I fall onto my knees and cover my ears HA! Not so easy, escape!
I twist in pain to see if the 'old man' can help.
The crown is veiled with rolling waves of cauldrons clouds
Through pain or shame, you turn away to hide
Or were you ever there, to shame!
From the edge of time
Time's timeless
Blame.

The Drowning of the Dogs
One careful caress
To sigh good-bye
Breathe deep
For one time, love must lie
And as you rest to sleep my friend
Breathe deep
For I must go and you must stay
Deep sleep
Beneath the oceans waves
For ever more
To caress our shore
For as the bubbles rise
To pop
Life's dying breath
Death's final lot.

The Evacuation of St. Kilda 1930 (August, Wednesday 29th)

Heersht......Heersht......Heersht
The weather is beautiful
Blue sky and calm green sea
The waves hiss across the beach
As wreathing snakes to kiss
Voices whisper as if some secret be
Maybe wake the old man's crown
Or Neptune in the sea.
The time is 7a.m.
The sun is climbing, as always
To go up, then down
AH! Really the sun never moves
'Tis us who spin around.
The thirty-six remaining people from St. Kilda
Board the H.M.S. Harebell.
The sound of the giant steel links wrestling with the capstan
Echoes around the stacs, setting white birds to flight
Swirling in circles like snows first blizzard
Sailors gaze up in amazement
The islanders stare with blank eyes, like statues,
As if all is a dream and they will wake any moment
And all will be as each good memory will recall.
The ship creeps from the Bay
A solitary chimney puffing smoke
Which weaves across the blue sky towards the mainland
A small rear gun points like a menacing finger at St. Kilda
To give cover from the island's claw-like stacs, In fear of reprisal.
I will never forget the islanders blank staring faces
As they stare back from the rear of the ship floating away
Like sheep on their last trip, peeping from limbo.
OH! There at the front of the ship
Like a figure head from the Titanic
Stands Finlay MacQueen, Proudly holding high, like a flag
The Last Great Auk.

Heersht......Heersht......Heersht

I stand alone upon the island
The peace is complete, for how long?
How long is a circle unless broken?
For will the games of war forget one harmless child.
I turn towards the village, no life.
I walk along the row of silent houses, like shells
Ghosts now will haunt
The dogs run around my legs
Lost spirits for ever earth-bound perplexed
I reach my hand gently towards them, to caress
AH! They cower and duck to hide
AH! They know of man's last lost trust
God bless you my four-legged friends
For the Lord moves in mysterious ways.
I walk into the schoolroom
There is a blackboard made from an old piece of floor linoleum
There are two different pews to seat fifteen children
On the wall is a 1930's calendar torn off at September
The small room smells of damp
And searches for the echoes from the ten departed children
A beetle crawls into an ink well busy with his new found home
While spiders wait as ever, for ever.
At one end of the schoolroom
Rests a collection box by a doorway
I wonder if one must pay to pass?
I fail to pass and walk outside where hangs a bell
The bell from the sunken Janet Cowan
Which kissed the rocks of St. Kilda in 1864
For whom the bell tolls, toll last for sunken dreams.
I walk into the houses which, moments past, were homes
Upon a table in each house a bible rests, and a small pile of oats
I wonder if another ship is to return on the next tide
with a new population for St. Kilda?
NO! Possibly gifts left for loved ones past ghosts?

I walk into my friend's house, No 2.

*Finlay has left the last broken Auk's egg
Resting on the open pages of his bible*

I look into his bible and the pages are open at

EXODUS

Heersht......Heersht......Heersht

Everything is peaceful and calm
The gentle waves stroke the beach
Lapping soft kisses of bliss.

I stare out at the ocean
The whispers have all gone
All the words have been spoken.

I...I...I suddenly hear a voice behind me

"Thank you Wordcatcher"

I quickly spin around
To find myself facing
Nothing
o
.

Heersht
/////////////////////////////////////
/////////////////////////////////
////////////////////////////
///////////////////////////////////////
Heersht

Sometimes shadows passed by
Memories lost, floating, brief,
A wind to blow lost green dreams
The breeze blown crisp brown leaf.

xxxx